POWER
POINTS

Other books by John Wimber with Kevin Springer
POWER EVANGELISM
POWER HEALING
POWER HEALING STUDY GUIDE

By Kevin Springer
POWER ENCOUNTERS

POWER POINTS

• YOUR ACTION PLAN TO: HEAR GOD'S
VOICE • BELIEVE GOD'S WORD • SEEK
THE FATHER • SUBMIT TO CHRIST • TAKE
UP THE CROSS • DEPEND ON THE HOLY
SPIRIT • FULFILL THE GREAT COMMISSION

John Wimber and Kevin Springer

HarperSanFrancisco
A Division of HarperCollinsPublishers

POWER POINTS: *Your Action Plan to: Hear God's Voice, Believe God's Word, Seek the Father, Submit to Christ, Take up the Cross, Depend on the Holy Spirit, Fulfill the Great Commission.* Copyright © 1991 by John Wimber and Kevin Springer. All rights reserved. Printed in the United States of America. No part of this book may be used or reproduced in any manner whatsoever without written permission except in the case of brief quotations embodied in critical articles and reviews. For information address HarperCollins Publishers, 10 East 53rd Street, New York, NY 10022.

FIRST EDITION

Library of Congress Cataloging-in-Publication Data

Wimber, John.
  Power points : your action plan to hear God's voice, believe God's
  word, seek the Father, submit to Christ, take up the cross, depend on the
  Holy Spirit, fulfill the Great Commission / John Wimber with Kevin
  Springer. — 1st ed.
    p.   cm.
  Includes bibliographical references and indexes.
  ISBN 0–06–069539–0
  1. Spiritual life. 2. Theology, Doctrinal—Popular works.
  I. Springer, Kevin. II. Title.
  BV4501.2.W5638 1991
  248.4—dc19   88-45685
                                                                    CIP

---

91 92 93 94 95 HAD 10 9 8 7 6 5 4 3 2 1

This edition is printed on acid-free paper that meets the American National Standards Institute Z39.48 Standard.

Dedicated to

Lawrance "Gunner" Payne

"A witness of Christ's sufferings and one
who also will share in the glory to be revealed"
1 Peter 5:1

CONTENTS

Contents

FOREWORD

by Michael Green

John Wimber is known throughout the Christian world and beyond. He has written two books that have had a phenomenal circulation. Why should he, of all people, need a foreword by anyone else—least of all myself? The answer is, of course, that he does not need it, but he has been gracious enough to invite me to contribute a few words, and I am delighted to accept.

Delighted because I believe John Wimber is frequently and unnecessarily misunderstood. He is thought of as "Mr. Signs and Wonders," and his two books *Power Evangelism* and *Power Healing,* might be construed as reinforcing that image. But Wimber is not a systematic theologian; he is a Christian leader who has hitherto brought his main artillery to bear against one of the most damaging weaknesses in Western Christianity, our deep-seated skepticism about the supernatural. He has attempted, with considerable success, to open our eyes to the seriousness of this crippling heresy. Consequently, he has laid particular emphasis on the signs of God's intervention and the wonders of his power in our own world of experience, if only we will trust him and open ourselves to his Holy Spirit.

But there is a lot more to John Wimber than that. In the past two years he has surprised some of his enthusiastic supporters by leading conferences on leadership, prayer, and holiness. And now he presents us with a book that reveals the roundedness and balance of the man. It is all about growth into spiritual maturity. It is positive and orthodox, generous and wide-ranging. He is disturbed at the enormous and accelerating erosion of Christianity in Western society in contrast to its remarkable growth in the Third World. He senses that hard times are coming, when external pressures upon the church will sweep aside a shallow Christianity. He sees around him in the church a sea of mindless enthusiasm on the one hand and dead orthodoxy on the other; neither makes for a spiritual maturity that can withstand the negative tendencies of the end of the twentieth century, let alone evangelize effectively within it.

So he has written this book to help people grow from their current (fashionable) individualism and relativism into spiritual maturity. It is by far the most fundamental of his books, for it deals with the great core elements in the Christian faith—the nature of the God we worship, what he has done for humankind, the way of holiness in the modern world, self-sacrifice, servanthood, and love.

Some will fancy that they detect here a new Wimber, more balanced, more reflective, more judicious. But those who know him well will see this book as the fruit of his own brokenness before God, his own inner growth, sacrifice, and humility.

The old emphases are still there, but set in a wider context. Spiritual gifts are rightly emphasized, but these are not toys or trophies for individual gratification; rather they are tools for the blessing of others. They are not character traits, but marks of the transcendent grace of God the Spirit among his people. All Christians have spiritual gifts: all Christians have been baptized by the Spirit at their conversion.

Evangelism is still given due prominence along with the spiritual gifts, which accompany its meteoric progress in the countries of the Third World, an area largely unaffected by Western skepticism about supernatural forces, good and evil. But this emphasis is balanced by a recognition that proclamation and demonstration of the good news belong together, that God's Spirit can never properly be divorced from his revelation, and that evangelism needs to be accompanied by a social involvement in the needs of hurting people. His own church in Anaheim, California, provides foster homes for babies of incarcerated women, ministry in many jails, and about a million meals for the homeless and destitute in the course of the year. Let those who criticize John Wimber for spiritual sensationalism take note!

Yes, the old emphases are still here, but they do not dominate the book. *Power Points* is written to instruct ignorant Christians about the basic truths of the faith; to challenge dull, orthodox Christians to expect great things from God; to teach shallow, experience-oriented Christians to understand the Fatherhood of God, the importance of the Trinity, the atonement, and revelation; and to stimulate complacent, run-of-the-mill Christians to strive after holiness, live in the power of the Spirit, and reach out with the gospel to the needy, Godless society all around us. It is astonishingly open and humble about the author's own struggles and failures. It is imbued with the spirit of sacrifice and servanthood. It is eminently readable and scrupulously biblical. It is all about the God of the Bible for today's world, in today's language.

If you are of a nit-picking disposition, there are theological hostages to fortune on every page: John Wimber is not a professional theologian. But if you read it as the author requests, stopping to reflect, pray, and apply personally what you read, this book will prove a great blessing. It is assured of a long future!

Michael Green
Regent College
July 1990
Vancouver, British Columbia

ACKNOWLEDGMENTS

This project took a year longer to complete than we anticipated. In part this was because of our concern to root our comments about spiritual growth in historical, orthodox theology. Therefore, we looked to several colleagues to read the manuscript in areas for which they have theological or pastoral training and experience. Their comments and insights were helpful. They include Dr. Peter Davids, professor of New Testament at Canadian Theological Seminary, Regina, Saskatchewan; Dr. Wayne A. Grudem, associate professor of biblical and systematic theology at Trinity Evangelical Divinity School, Deerfield, Illinois; Dr. Don Williams, pastor of the Vineyard of the Coast, San Diego, California; Dr. Jack Deere, associate pastor of the Anaheim Vineyard Christian Fellowship, Anaheim, California; Dr. Richard Nathan, pastor of the Vineyard Christian Fellowship of Columbus, Ohio; Dr. Richard J. Foster, professor of theology at Friends University, Wichita, Kansas; Dr. Alan Cole, Trinity Theological College, Singapore; and Kevin Perrotta, managing editor of *Faith & Renewal* journal, Ann Arbor, Michigan.

John C. Blattner, editor of *Faith & Renewal,* Ann Arbor, Michigan, read every page of our last draft and suggested changes that greatly improved the book.

There were others who encouraged us and in several instances they allowed stories from their own lives to be used as illustrations in the text. They include Lawrance "Gunner" Payne, Pacific City, Oregon; Michael and Rosemary Green, Vancouver, British Columbia; and C. Peter Wagner, Pasadena, California.

All biblical quotations are taken from the New International Version (NIV), unless otherwise indicated.

John Wimber
Kevin Springer
July 1990
Yorba Linda, California

PART I

Dynamics of Spiritual Growth

I

Power Points

We all know what it means to grow physically. Like most parents, Carol and I* frequently measured our four children's heights as they were growing up. From year to year we charted their growth with pencil marks and dates on a corner by the kitchen doorway. We were amazed to see dramatic changes as the kids went through growth spurts.

Spiritual growth is more difficult to define and chart than physical growth. But I think it can be summed up in one statement: *spiritual growth is the process we go through here on earth of becoming more Christlike.*

The goal of spiritual growth is more than just improved behavior. Self-help programs *improve* people; God's intent is to *transform* us into replicas of his Son.[1] If maturity were merely improved behavior, we could grow toward maturity by reading some of the hundreds of self-help books available today. But because God's goal is our transformation, the creation of new men and women, spiritual growth is different from a self-help program.

---

* Unless otherwise noted, the "I" in the text is John Wimber.

3

The Way of Maturity

Spiritual growth is a *process*. Scripture says that we are being transformed "into his likeness with ever-increasing glory" (2 Cor. 3:18). Spiritual growth happens in stages. Paul and the author of the Letter to the Hebrews both talk about baby Christians needing one type of spiritual food—milk—and mature Christians needing another—solid food (1 Cor. 3:2; Heb. 5:12–13; see also 1 Pet. 2:2).

This process will not be completed until Christ's Second Coming (1 Cor. 15:35–58), though much of it happens here on earth. Even mature Christians, then, are nevertheless *growing* Christians (2 Cor. 3:18; Phil. 3:12–15; Col. 1:10). This is where the analogy with physical growth breaks down. Adults reach full height, a point beyond which they will grow no taller. But Christians never reach a point beyond which they cannot still grow. So the teaching in this book is for you, no matter which stage you are at right now—whether you are a new convert needing the basics of spiritual growth, a young Christian wishing to grow to maturity, or a long-time believer wanting to go ever deeper into the spiritual life.

Eureka Moments

The process of spiritual growth is punctuated by certain crucial moments that I call *power points*. These power points are based on our interaction with the objective markers of core Christian truths that direct us toward maturity; if we follow them well, they change the direction of our lives.

They change the direction of our lives by first changing us. They change the way we think about God, ourselves, and people around us. They also change the way we live. At each point we become a little more like Jesus, reflecting some new aspect of his character in our character and actions.

I use the term "power points" because there are or can be eureka moments when we know—*really know*—some key truth of the Christian life. These are points in time in which understanding and experience come together. "Eureka" means any exclamation of triumphant achievement, equivalent to I've got it! I've mastered it. I've understood it!" *That's what a power point is—an "I've got it!" time in our relationship with God.*

Thought of this way, power points are more than the objective markers along the path of spiritual growth: they are experiences of God's truth that boost us along, that catapult us toward maturity. Power points raise our vision and sense of calling. Elevated vision in turn creates an expectant, highly motivated environment. Those who experience power points *want* to take on new spiritual challenges—and as a result they grow.

Power points are rooted in objective truth about God, which keeps us on a sure path toward maturity. They are like the pitons, or metal spikes, that mountain climbers rely on for safety when they scale steep, rocky cliffs.

As the climbers move up the mountain, they plant the pitons firmly in rock. The lead climber passes rope through them. The rope is attached to the climber below as well as the lead climber. Should the lead climber fall off the cliff, he will remain attached to the piton and climber below, thus not falling to his death. With this system (called belaying), climbers can never fall too far from where they last planted a piton.

Knowing Jesus puts us on the mountain—on the path to maturity. But to grow, we need to continue climbing and planting pitons. It is good to know, though, that, if we slip, the last piton is always there, and Jesus is the climber below holding our rope.

Believing about God

Spiritual growth and personal transformation involve growth in faith. The heart of each power point is biblical truth. Without growth in knowledge *about* God, our experiences will have no lasting effect. This is the content side of faith—who God is, what he has done and is doing, what the nature and purpose of humanity is, and so on.

Several years ago I was invited to lead a Bible study group in a local hospital. Having introduced myself and my topic for the evening, I was interrupted by one of the participants: "I don't wanna hear no doctrine," he said, "I just want you to teach the Bible." For him, the study of "doctrine" was boring and unrelated to the Bible. He thought doctrine was "men's ideas" and opposed to God's word. But Christian doctrine is rooted in Scripture.

The idea that biblical truth and rational thinking are opposed to one another is a gross misunderstanding of Christianity. As T. C. Hammond writes, "There is no biblical opposition between 'faith' and 'understanding' or 'knowledge'. . ."[2] In Colossians 1:10 Paul says that a life fully pleasing to God is one that is continually "growing in the knowledge of God" (see also 2 Pet. 1:5).

Growth in faith and obedience builds on our intellectual grasp of the content of Christian belief. Still, it is not enough just to *know* doctrine; our lives must be *submitted* to it. Let me illustrate this with a hypothetical story about the president of the United States. The president frequently travels abroad to meet with world leaders. But even while away he is still responsible for leading the country. I imagine the White House staff back in Washington receive a constant flow of directives from him, telling them to prepare reports, hire and fire personnel, reorganize departments, and meet with lawmakers to discuss any number of issues. How would the president react if, upon returning from one of his trips, he discovered no action had been taken on any of his directives? What if, instead, his subordinates told him, "Mr. President, we read all your memos. We called committee meetings to discuss them. We even did linguistic studies to make sure we understood them correctly. We concluded that they were mighty fine memos, full of wisdom." I think the president would be more interested in his subordinates *fulfilling* his words. The Lord, too, is as interested in our actions as he is in what we know. *Faith is a matter of what we do* (James 2:18, 26; 3:13).

Believing in God

The experience side of faith is believing *in* God. We have a person-to-person relationship with him that is characterized by intimacy: trust, dependence, giving ourselves fully to God—in sum, having a *personal* encounter with him (John 17:3).

Belief in God is a matter of the disposition of the heart. In Scripture the "heart" refers not to the organ that pumps blood, but to the core, the epicenter, of one's being. It is possible for us to verbalize faith but be far from the Lord in the disposition of our hearts: "These people honor me with their lips, but their hearts are far from me" (Matt. 15:8). Sometimes we can find out more about what we believe by how we live than by what we confess.

I once heard it suggested in reference to John 8:32—"Then you will know the truth, and the truth will set you free"—that truth *in itself* sets us free. But this is not what Jesus teaches. We need to read a previous verse in the passage to understand what Jesus means. "To the Jews who had believed him, Jesus said, 'If you hold to my teaching, you are really my disciples'" (v. 31). Jesus says that to really "know" the truth is not just to believe it, but also to *obey* it. "Christianity is truth," William Barclay writes, "but it is truth in action."[3] That is belief *in* God. Before I was saved, the truth was available but I did not know it; it was of no benefit to me. Paul says that God recognized David as a man after his own heart because "he will *do* everything I want him to do" (Acts 13:22). It is the truth that we *know and do* that frees us.

2

Word and Spirit

Over the years I have observed that Christians tend to fall into two camps: subjectivists and rationalists. Subjectivists emphasize experience, sometimes at the expense of knowledge of the Bible. Rationalists, in a never-ending search for "objective truth," are suspicious of spiritual experience. Their fear of experience can leave them spiritually dry. Both extremes are wrong. Both detach experience and truth, which are meant to go together. Subjectivists can fall into the trap of seeking experience for its own sake. Rationalists can become tied to a corpse of dead orthodoxy, studying the Bible yet somehow avoiding knowing the God who wrote it (John 5:37).

Martyn Lloyd-Jones says that dead orthodoxy "is the greatest danger confronting the individual who is evangelical in his outlook, as it is indeed the greatest danger confronting any individual church or groups of churches that can be described as evangelical."[1] Lloyd-Jones points out two damaging characteristics of dead orthodoxy.

First, dead orthodoxy produces smug self-satisfaction in people; they are defensive about their faith and rarely take risks with God:

> There is nothing vital in the religion and in the worship of such
> people. They expect nothing, and they get nothing, and nothing
> happens to them. They go to God's house, not with the idea of

meeting with God, not with the idea of waiting upon him. It never crosses their minds, or enters into their hearts that something may happen in the service. . . . The idea that God may suddenly visit his people, and descend upon them, the whole thrill of being in the presence of God, and sensing his nearness, and his power, never even enters their imaginations.[2]

This leads to the second damaging characteristic of dead orthodoxy, "a dislike of enthusiasm . . . [which] can be one of the greatest hindrances of all to revival."[3] Lloyd-Jones cautions that in our enthusiasm we must avoid confusion, a worked-up sense of joy, and emotionalism. But fear of excesses can create an over-reaction. For example, trying to ensure that everything is done decently and in good order, churches can become overly formalized and ritualized, in stark contrast to the spontaneous, lively meetings described in the New Testament.

God's revelation must penetrate our hearts in order to change how we live. The analogy of a match and oxygen captures the dynamic relationship between the two. A match will remain lit only if sufficient oxygen is present to feed its flame. If oxygen is in short supply, the flame will have no staying power. Information about God is like the match; spiritual experience is like the oxygen. We need both.

When experience of God is separated from knowledge about God, people fall into various errors: Eastern mysticism, pantheism, even the occult. When revelation is defined as information alone, we are left with dead orthodoxy—the equating of Christianity with intellectual assent to creedal statements and core doctrines.

The Marks of Maturity

We need clarity about Christian maturity to avoid falling into subjectivism or rationalism. Too often when we talk about spiritual maturity we speak in vague terms. We talk of "loving one another" or "being holy." Rarely do we paint a detailed picture of what that means in practical terms. But people who have vague notions about mature Christian behavior often develop nagging feelings of inadequacy and guilt rather than new attitudes and behavior.

Scripture spells out in specific terms what God is looking for. For example, 1 Peter gives a general commandment: "As obedient children, do not conform to the evil desires you had when you lived in ignorance. But just as he who called you is holy, so be holy in all you do; for it is written: 'Be holy, because I am holy'" (1 Pet. 1:14–16). This general precept is accompanied by operational instructions:

> [R]id yourselves of all malice and all deceit, hypocrisy, envy, and slander of every kind. . . . [L]ive as servants of God. Show proper respect to everyone: Love the brotherhood of believers, fear God, honor the king. . . . Finally, all of you, live in harmony with one another; be sympathetic, love as brothers, be compassionate and humble. Do not repay evil with evil or insult with insult, but with blessing, because to this you were called so that you may inherit a blessing. For, "Whoever would love life and see good days must keep his tongue from evil and his lips from deceitful speech. He must turn from evil and do good; he must seek peace and pursue it.". . . Always be prepared to give an answer to everyone who asks you to give the reason for the hope that you have. (1 Pet. 2:1, 16–17; 3:8–11, 15–16)

I will try to cover some of the key power points along the path to spiritual maturity and outline the basic characteristics of Christian maturity for each one, with suggestions of how we can grow into them. Whenever we lay out specific behavior norms we run the risk of trying to obey God in our own strength, without reliance on Christ to empower us (Gal. 2:20) or the Holy Spirit to change us (Gal. 5:22–23). So I remind you that Christian maturity is a fruit of the Spirit. The fruit of the Spirit comes from the Holy Spirit working through a repentant, born-again heart. The outward flow of the Spirit's inward working produces thoughts and actions that are godly and mature.

This truth was impressed upon me when I was only ten years old. At that time my family lived in Illinois. Our household consisted of my mother, stepfather, grandmother, and myself. Those were difficult times financially, and we were forced to live in an economically depressed area.

One day a demolition crew came and began tearing down the homes across the street. I went over and asked one of the crew members why he was destroying everything. "We're getting rid of the slums so we can build new housing," he told me.

Slums? I lived in the slums? I went home and announced to my mother, "We are *poor!*"

"No," she responded, "we're not poor. We just don't have a lot of money. Poor is in your head. It's the way you look at yourself. And we're not poor!"

In time a new housing development replaced the old houses, and the old families from the neighborhood moved back in. A short time later we moved away from the neighborhood, but not before I saw the new buildings abused and run down. Even though I was only a young boy, I concluded that you can change people's surroundings, but if you do not change the people themselves, their surroundings will soon reflect their inner state. Mom was right. One of the roots of poverty is in the heart. People must be changed from the inside out.

Habits of Righteousness

So, what does a mature Christian look like? Here is the definition of spiritual maturity I will adopt in this book: *A mature Christian is one who has developed habits of righteousness in relationship to God, to self, and to other people. All of this is accomplished on the foundation of the word of God and through the power of Christ and the Holy Spirit.*

Habits of righteousness in relationship to God are concerned with such things as obedience, repentance, hearing God's voice, caring for the poor, and the disciplines of prayer, meditation, fasting, Scripture study, and perseverance (see Matt. 6:1–18).

Talking about our relationship to our self means talking about our character. Paul summarizes some of the key Christian characteristics in his description of the fruit of the Spirit—"Love, joy, peace, patience, kindness, goodness faithfulness, gentleness and self-control" (Gal. 5:22–23). The different elements of the fruit of the Spirit are the virtues of Christ, which cover such issues as humility, emotional stability, and taking responsibility for living a holy life.

Spiritual maturity is also demonstrated in relationships with others—in showing loyalty, godly speech patterns, peacemaking, and so on.

The last area—our relationship to others—warrants further comment. One of the most damaging characteristics of the Western church is the hurtful way Christians sometimes treat one another. As I grow older I am becoming more sensitive to the damage that disunity and malicious criticism do to the witness of Christ in the world. Simply stated, too many Christians have never learned to love each other. Graciousness, forgiveness, and self-restraint must begin in the house of God; and God's house is bigger than any particular room we may inhabit within it!

The authors of Scripture wrote about spiritual maturity as though it were attainable for all Christians. They presented God's call to us as, "I'm calling you on, because I know you can do it *with my help!*" That gives me hope. When I consider the biblical portrait of mature behavior, I find it easy to become discouraged. The standards are so high. It is easy to think, "I can't make it." But we *are* each called to maturity, and with God's help we *can* grow toward it. We should not expect or hope for *perfection* today or tomorrow or next week, but we should always expect and hope for *growth* day by day (Rom. 6:19).

My hope and prayer, as you cover the power points outlined in this book, is best expressed in Paul's words in Philippians 3:12–17:

> Not that I . . . have already been made perfect, but I press on to
> take hold of that for which Christ Jesus took hold of me. Brothers
> [and sisters], I do not consider myself yet to have taken hold of it.
> But one thing I do: Forgetting what is behind and straining toward

what is ahead, I press on toward the goal to win the prize for which God has called me heavenward in Christ Jesus.

All of us who are mature should take such a view of things. And if on some point you think differently, that too God will make clear to you. Only let us live up to what we have already attained.

Join with others in following my example, brothers [and sisters], and take note of those who live according to the pattern we gave you.

Throughout this chapter I have referred to the word of God as the foundation for Christian experience and spiritual growth. So it should come as no surprise that the word of God is our first power point.

PART II

Hearing God's Voice

3

God in the Desert

Las Vegas, Nevada, is the gambling capital of the world. Its neon-lit landscape is also dotted with marriage chapels where couples—who in some instances have known each other only a few hours—can get married in ten minutes. Divorces can be obtained almost as readily. In short, Las Vegas is not a good place to be living when your marriage is collapsing.

But that is where I was living in 1961, when my wife, Carol, phoned me to suggest that I look into a sixty-day, Las Vegas "no-fault" divorce. Neither of us were Christians. A few weeks before she had asked me to leave home, which was in Westminster, California. I moved 250 miles to Las Vegas to fulfill a casino contract as a musician. Our three sons remained with her. Even though I loved Carol and the children, I knew our relationship had deteriorated badly.

Later that week I told a fellow band member about my problems. "Why don't you go out in the desert and experience the sunrise?" he suggested. "It's a great experience." I had never been all that interested in sunrises, but I was in such despair that I decided to take his advice. I hopped in the car and took off.

On the way out to the desert I suddenly began weeping uncontrollably. I was overwhelmed by Someone or Something—whatever it was, I did not know. I pulled my car over and got out. In my pain, I looked up to the star-filled heavens and cried out, "If there is anyone there, help me!" Immediately I felt self-conscious and embarrassed—even though no one had witnessed my crying out. "Oh, no," I thought. "I'm talking to the dark. I'm going crazy."

But when I got back to my hotel I found a message from Carol, asking me to call her. "Come and get me," she said. "I want to try one more time to make the marriage work." I was astonished. Only hours before I had cried out to the heavens—and now this! Smugly, I thought, "I'm in touch with the supernatural!"

I jumped in my car and drove back to Westminster, talking all the way to the Someone or Something I had shouted to in the desert. Carol had been adamant about the divorce; in fact, she had been unwilling even to talk with me. I knew a force bigger than me had changed her mind. Could that force be God? "Hot dog," I said. "You got her to change her mind!" That is how my prayer life began. I had a lot to learn about God (and about marriage)!

I did not know that during this time Carol had been asking God what was causing our marriage to go wrong. On the same day as my desert experience she received a scriptural insight into our relationship. In a way she couldn't explain, she suddenly became sure that our marriage was being attacked. She had only a rudimentary understanding of God, and she knew even less about the devil. But somehow she *knew* that something evil was attacking us. This insight was enough for her to give the marriage one more chance.

Many people—Christians and non-Christians alike—have had a similar experience—a sudden awareness that "Something is out there," a sense of purpose that pointed to a Creator, a feeling that there was a battle going on around them that had eternal implications. Such experiences come through a variety of means and circumstances: personal crises and the glory of nature are two common ones. We should not be surprised that God reveals himself to us in this way, for the Bible states clearly that God makes himself known to us, even when we deny him (Rom. 1:18–23).

To understand what happened to me in the desert, and to Carol back in California, we must understand how God speaks to men and women. In other words, we must tackle the biblical doctrine of revelation.

Revelation

Christianity is a revealed religion. The term "revelation" refers to God's self-disclosure to men and women. It is translated from a Greek word that means the drawing back of a veil to reveal hidden things. That is what the God of the Bible does: he reveals himself to us so that we may know him, love him, and serve him.

One writer defines revelation as "knowledge that comes to us from outside ourselves and [that is] beyond our own ability to discover."[1] How can finite minds penetrate the nature of an infinite God? How can the clay pot understand the mind of its potter? Clearly the only way we know anything about God is because he first graciously chooses to reveal himself to us.

Some people have tried through philosophical reasoning to prove God's existence. For example, they argue that since everything must have a beginning (or cause), and since creation could not have created itself, there must be a First Cause: namely, God. While this kind of exercise helps make belief in God more reasonable, the fact is we can never "prove" anything about God through human reason. Without God's gracious act of self-disclosure we can know little of his nature and how to have a relationship with him. Helpful though "proofs" may be in pointing people toward God, they do not prove God's existence. Only God's own revelation does that.

Paul writes, "I want you to know, brothers, that the gospel I preached is not something that man made up. I did not receive it from any man, nor was I taught it; rather, I received it by revelation from Jesus Christ" (Gal. 1:11–12). The gospel, the good news—the core of information about God and what it means to be a Christian—is received (experienced) by revelation, by the self-disclosure of a holy God to sinful men and women.

4

A Thirst for the Knowledge of God

Theologians generally speak of two kinds of revelation. The first is called "general revelation," and it comes in three ways.

First, there is a testimony to God's existence in *creation* itself: "The heavens declare the glory of God; the skies proclaim the work of his hands. Day after day they pour forth speech; night after night they display knowledge" (Ps. 19:1–2; see also Ps. 97:6; Rom. 1:18–20).

Second, we are given *consciences* on which the distinction between right and wrong is engraved by God:

> Indeed, when Gentiles, who do not have the law, do by nature things required by the law, they are a law for themselves, even though they do not have the law, since they show that the requirements of the law are written on their hearts, their consciences also bearing witness, and their thoughts now accusing, now even defending them. (Rom. 2:14–15)

Finally, general revelation comes through God's continuing *providence*. His fatherly care in "giving . . . rain from heaven and crops

in their seasons" (Acts 14:17) and overseeing the rise and fall of
nations (Acts 17:26–28) provides signs that point toward himself.

The Bible says that all men and women receive general revelation, and that it is sufficient to make us aware that there is a God
(Rom. 1:20). When I look back on my desert experience, I now understand that the Something I sensed there was God. I sensed he was
as eager to know me as I was to know him. This was a power point
in my life, an experience that changed my attitude toward God.

But while general revelation is a powerful witness of God's presence and reveals something of his character, it does not tell us how
our sins can be forgiven or how we can be saved (Rom. 10:14–17).
If the only knowledge I ever had about God came from my desert
experience, I would be left groping around in the dark and seeking
after "spiritual experiences." Carol, conscious of the devil and of evil,
would have been doomed to a life of fear. Without knowledge of
Jesus Christ's victory over sin and Satan at the cross, Carol and I
would have been conscious of our need for salvation—but we would
have had no hope of attaining it.

General revelation is a sort of divine carrot that draws us along
a path toward Jesus Christ. When I experienced the desert sunrise
outside Las Vegas, I discovered something greater than myself, but
I did not have a clue about what it could be. This need to know
what or who it was became an insatiable thirst for a deeper knowledge of God.

Questions

From this point Carol and I began talking about God all the time.
Who was he? How did he operate? Could we know him? Anyone
who raises such questions is soon aware of the need for authoritative answers. This posed a problem for us. Neither of us had
any church affiliation as adults; in fact, my family had never had any
church affiliation at all. Carol's family had been Catholic, and she
remembered enough about her childhood religious experiences to
know that people who wanted to learn about God should read the

Bible. She went out and purchased a *New English Bible New Testament* and we began reading it. But we found it difficult to understand.

We were committed to getting our marriage working right, and we knew that Las Vegas was not a good environment for family life. So, in the summer of 1961, we left Las Vegas and returned to Orange County.

Carol soon learned she was pregnant with our fourth child. As so often happens with young families, we decided we needed to find a church and a religious school to provide the children with moral teaching. Since the only church background we had was Carol's childhood Catholicism, we decided to start there.

I began taking instruction in the Catholic faith. We renewed our wedding vows because our first marriage was not recognized as valid by the Catholic church, and it was important to Carol that our marriage receive the church's blessing. Carol also went to confession around this time, and as a result a major healing occurred in her life. To this day she does not understand the full implications of what happened at her confession, but she knows God forgave her and used it to bring her closer to him.

My time of instruction in the Catholic faith did not work out too well, however. In part, this was because the priest with whom I met was struggling with his own problems. He had recently suffered a breakdown of some sort; he appeared to be in a crisis of faith and could not handle my questions—not that they were particularly probing. Our discussions reached a point where he insisted that I drop my questions and uncritically accept the authority of the church and the Bible. (I did not understand until years later how important the concept of the authority of the church was to him.) I responded by asking another question; he boiled over and threw me out of his office. This, I thought, ended my search for God.

In November 1962, however, some old friends reappeared in our lives. We had known Dick and Lynn Heying for many years. Dick and I had played together in several bands (he was a drummer). As couples we had spent many evenings together partying. But now there was something different about them. They no longer wanted to party, and they appeared to be very happy. Little did we know that Dick and Lynn had become Christians and were praying for us. Dick began to drop by the house weekly to talk with me about his newfound relationship with Jesus. Also during this time Lynn frequently talked with Carol on the phone.

Dick told me about Lawrance "Gunner" Payne, a Bible teacher who was coming to their house in nearby Yorba Linda each week and answering all their questions about God. By April of 1963 Carol and I were interested in attending one of Gunner's Bible studies. We were impressed by how the Heyings' lives had changed. And we were eager to meet someone who could answer all *our* questions.

But there was one problem: I was self-conscious about showing my ignorance of God and the Bible to the twenty-five people who regularly attended their group. I could not stand the thought of embarrassing myself in front of them! Carol was farther along in her spiritual pilgrimage. She wanted the answer to only one question: Who is Jesus Christ? She did not care what others thought of her spirituality. The large group met on Tuesday evenings, which was my only night off, so I thought it would not be possible to study the Bible with Gunner. But when I told Dick I could not attend and why, he phoned back later to say they had switched their Tuesday meeting to Monday night and that he, Gunner, Lynn, Carol, and I could now meet on Tuesday evenings! How could we refuse such a small group?

I was not an ideal Bible study group member. The first night I fell into a chair in the corner of the living room, lit up a cigarette, and announced, "I have a few questions before we get started." Then I began asking Gunner all the questions I had asked so many times before: How do you know the Bible is true? How do you know there is a God? Why are you doing this? What do you get out of it? Does the church pay you to do this?

Gunner patiently answered each question and noted, "You sure are hungry." I said, "No, I'm not hungry. I ate before I came." I did not understand that Gunner was speaking of spiritual hunger. Then I assaulted him with more questions. I was becoming obsessed with learning about God. Gunner's patience was remarkable, and after the first night I never questioned his sincerity.

These weekly meetings, which frequently lasted well past midnight, went on for three months. Week in and week out we asked our questions, and Gunner took us to the Scriptures to search for answers. Carol and I also began reading the Bible on our own, and for the first time it was making some sense to us.

From the outset I knew there was something different about Gunner Payne. He was a good teacher—intelligent, insightful, patient. But that was not what caught my attention. What impressed me was the quality of the man, his character: he appeared to be sound, complete, uncorrupted. Nothing mattered to him except living for God; the peace of Jesus permeated his being.

Gunner's character was more important to me than his knowledge of the Bible. I needed a trustworthy witness to Christ, and Gunner filled the bill. Gunner's *life* was revelation; the way he lived embodied the gospel. For a time Gunner Payne was the principal means through which God spoke to me. I wanted to know what it was that created such peace within him, so I listened to what he said.

After we had been attending the Bible study group for a few weeks, I walked into our kitchen one morning, and Carol announced that she had learned the answer to her question. "John," she said, "Jesus is the Son of God. Do you hear me? I now see that Jesus is the Son of God." "Yeah," I thought, "and Chicago is in Illinois. So what?" I still did not comprehend the significance of Jesus Christ.

"But that changes everything," Carol said. "It means there is something that we need to do!" She didn't understand *what* she needed to do about this new piece of information, but she was sure it meant that she needed to do *something,* and that she would soon know what it was.

We continued to attend the Bible studies, sometimes driving in hours early just to be in Yorba Linda, because we thought God resided there. We also came early to visit Gunner at his welding shop and ask more questions. At one point Carol and I told Gunner that we wanted to sign up to get whatever he had. We asked him what we needed to do. He said, "It's too soon. You're not ready yet. Premature births don't produce healthy children. Apples fall when they're ripe."

5

Special Revelation

General revelation prepared Carol and me for a fuller revelation, one that is rooted in the Bible and communicated through the Holy Spirit, by which *God reveals who he is and how we may have communion with him*. Theologians call this "special revelation." It is humbling for me to realize that I can know God only if *he* chooses to make himself known to me! The fact that he chooses me, reveals himself, and initiates our relationship continues to astound me.

God reveals himself through the things he *does*. The God of the Bible is the Lord of history. He dealt with Israel and with surrounding nations in the Middle East. God performed miracles and acts of mighty power to reveal his righteousness and grace to Israel. He delivered the Israelites from Egyptian bondage, brought them through forty years of wilderness wandering, and led them into the promised land of Canaan. He gave them the Mosaic Law, established their worship, disciplined them, loved them—in other words, he revealed himself to them (Deut. 29:29).

But God's revelation is more than just his actions. Revelation also includes the *interpretation* of those actions. I think of it like a mathematical formula: A + I = R. Action plus Interpretation equals Revelation. Those who are gifted and commissioned to interpret God's actions and express his mind are called prophets. The Bible says, "Surely the Sovereign Lord does nothing without revealing his plan to his servants the prophets" (Amos 3:7).[1]

We need the prophets' interpretation of biblical events for the full disclosure of their meaning. The Exodus had more meaning to the Israelites than simply relief from Egyptian bondage. The Ten Commandments begin by reminding the nation of Israel that it was God who brought them up out of Egypt. Time and again the Old Testament records God's acts of salvation: "the Lord, who brought you up out of Egypt with mighty power and outstretched arm, is the one you must worship" (2 Kings 17:36). Historic events revealed God's nature and created faith throughout the nation of Israel. God told them through the prophets that the events pointed toward a future salvation, toward a Messiah who would redeem them and establish the fullness of the kingdom of God.

This Messiah came as God's fullest revelation in history: the incarnation of Jesus Christ, the Son of God (Gal. 4:4). John's Gospel says, "The Word [Jesus] became flesh and made his dwelling among us" (John 1:14). The author of the Letter to the Hebrews says:

> In the past God spoke to our forefathers through the prophets at many times and in various ways, but in these last days he has spoken to us by his Son, whom he appointed heir of all things, and through whom he made the universe. The Son is the radiance of God's glory and the exact representation of his being, sustaining all things by his powerful word. (Heb. 1:1–3)

The apostle John refers to Jesus as the Word of God:

> In the beginning was the Word, and the Word was with God, and the Word was God. . . . The Word became flesh and made his dwelling among us. We have seen his glory, the glory of the One and Only, who came from the Father, full of grace and truth. . . . No one has ever seen God, but God the One and Only, who is at the Father's side, has made him known. (John 1:1, 14, 18)

John's point is simple: the Person of Jesus Christ is the apex of God's revelation. He was a real, historical figure who performed many signs and wonders that authenticated his claims—among them, that he came from the Father, which was an implicit claim to deity (John 20:30–31; Matt. 11:2–6). Jesus is the only perfect revelation of the Father, and salvation is found exclusively in him. Only those who trust in the risen Lord are saved (Rom. 10:9); only those who acknowledge that Jesus came in the flesh are of God (1 John 4:2).

Do you want to know the heavenly Father? Then look at his Son, Jesus Christ, because he came to reveal his Father's nature to us. As Jesus said to Philip, "Anyone who has seen me has seen the Father" (John 14:9). When we say, "Lord, show us the Father," God's answer to us is the same as it was to Philip: look at Jesus.

The Bible and Revelation

Most Christians automatically associate the word of God with the Bible, the Old and New Testaments. And well they should, for the written record reveals the incarnate Word of God. To reach all men and women, God provided a written record of his mighty acts. How else could succeeding generations know about his Son, Jesus Christ? He wanted to ensure an accurate historical record and authentic interpretation of his acts, so there could be no misunderstanding about his nature and how to know him. God did this in the Bible, and through it all men and women may learn about and benefit from God's dealings with Israel and also from the life of Christ.

The Bible is special revelation. If we want to know what God thinks, we must know what the Bible says. When I became convinced the Bible was the word of God and submitted to it, my life was changed. I knew I could no longer stand in judgment upon Scripture, discarding teaching I could not accept and submitting only to those ideas that conformed to *my* idea of truth. I realized the Bible was written in such a manner that to reject one part was to reject it all. This was a power point, a discovery that put me on the narrow path to salvation.

Some of you may be wondering about a question I asked Gunner Payne: "How do we know the Bible is true?" I will try to answer that and other questions about the Bible in Part III.

PART III

Believing God's Word

6

Why Believe the Bible?

You may find it hard to believe how ignorant I was of the Bible in my preconversion days. But I was raised in what church growth experts call the pagan pool—no discernible church involvement, no discussion of God, no significant interest of any kind in spiritual things. I am not alone. Today approximately seventy-eight million American adults have no church identity.[1] Almost no one in my family for four generations had any kind of church affiliation.

So the first time I read the Bible I had no way of knowing its benefits or understanding what it meant. You may have been raised in a home that assumed the Bible was true, beneficial, and understandable. As a result of your upbringing, you believe these things are true. But you may not know *why* they are true. Understanding and accepting these basic truths about the Bible is a prerequisite to spiritual growth, because special revelation comes to us from the Bible and through the guidance of the Holy Spirit.

In Chapter 5, I wrote that special revelation is embodied in the Bible as the word of God. The Scriptures attest to God's prophetic word, his works in history, and the interpretation of his works. If the Bible is not wholly true, then our faith sinks in a murky bog of subjectivism. If there is no objective record of God's nature and work,

31

who is to say that Christians' experience and understanding of God is more reliable than the experiences of Hindus or Muslims? The Bible is our primary source of the knowledge of God, our guide for faith and practice in the Christian life.

The Authority of Scripture

The Bible has a unique authority, derived from God himself. This is verified by two witnesses. First, the Bible itself has an air of authority unlike any other book's. Second, God through the Holy Spirit testifies in the reader's heart that it is his truth.

The Bible consists of the Old and New Testaments. The Old Testament, with thirty-nine books, was written in Hebrew and Aramaic. The last book—Malachi—was completed about 433 B.C. The New Testament, written in Greek between A.D. 50 and 100, consists of twenty-seven books. Beginning in the first century, the books were slowly collected and read in the churches, depending on which books a given church had; later church leaders examined them closely and compared them with other books that were being circulated, books some were claiming to be divinely inspired.

By the end of the fourth century there developed agreement throughout the church about the *canon,* the list of books that belong in the Bible. "Canon" comes from a Greek word that means "measuring rod" or "rule." When applied to Scripture, "canon" indicates a collection of books that have passed the test of inspiration. It also indicates that the books themselves are the "rule of faith," objective truth by which all doctrine is tested.

It is important to remember that the books of the New Testament were considered authoritative before they were formally recognized. Placing them on an approved list did not make them more authoritative, for the nature of the books themselves and the authority of the writers were all that was needed. I have heard it said that the Bible is not an authorized collection of books, but a collection of authorized books. Or, as J. I. Packer says, "The Church no more gave us the New Testament canon than Sir Isaac Newton gave us the force of gravity. God gave us gravity, by his work of creation, and similarly he gave us the New Testament canon, by inspiring the individual books that make it up."[2] While church recognition of the canon is not the basis for the Bible's authority, it does testify to the Bible's intrinsic power and authority. For nineteen hundred years a continual stream of people have been converted to Christ after reading or hearing Scripture.

One of the chief reasons for believing that Scripture is the word of God is that Jesus himself clearly treated it that way. Consider Christ's attitude toward the Bible. First, *Jesus viewed Scripture as his final authority in matters of truth and ethics*. During a controversy with Jewish leaders he said, "the Scripture cannot be broken" (John 10:35). And he rebuked the devil with the words, "It is written . . ." (Matt. 4:1–11). In refuting the Pharisees and Sadducees Jesus used the Scriptures as a basis of authority, and his own teaching was always rooted in Scripture (Mark 7:6–13).

Second, *Jesus held and taught an exceedingly high view of Scripture*. He heard God's voice speaking through the words of Scripture. In Matthew 5:17–19 he said,

> "Do not think that I have come to abolish the Law or the Prophets; I have not come to abolish them but to fulfill them. I tell you the truth, until heaven and earth disappear, not the smallest letter, not the least stroke of a pen, will by any means disappear from the Law until everything is accomplished. Anyone who breaks one of the least of these commandments and teaches others to do the same will be called least in the kingdom of heaven, but whoever practices and teaches these commands will be called great in the kingdom of heaven."

To Jesus the whole of Scripture is of one piece, every part of it the word of God. If Jesus had this view of Scripture, should we not also? The disciples who had been with Jesus had the same attitude toward the New Testament books (2 Pet. 3:15–16). Moreover, they were conscious of writing revelation rather than mere human opinion (1 Cor. 14:37).

Revelation of Jesus

This leads to the most fundamental reason for believing the Bible is the word of God: the Holy Spirit testifies in our hearts that Jesus, who is the focus of Scripture, reveals God to us. Through the work of the Holy Spirit the written word is translated into the dynamic word of God, making Scripture meaningful to us as the Spirit illumines our minds. The testimony of the Holy Spirit is an act of God's grace. Not all men and women respond to the authority of Scripture, perhaps simply because they have not received illumination from the Holy Spirit, or perhaps because they have rejected the Spirit's illumination. Paul says, "The man without the Spirit does not accept the things that come from the Spirit of God, for they are foolishness to him, and he cannot understand them, because they are spiritually discerned" (1 Cor. 2:14).

At the Last Supper, Jesus told the disciples, "But when he, the Spirit of truth, comes, he will guide you into all truth" (John 16:13). The Holy Spirit helps us welcome the truth of God in our lives. He enlivens our hearts to understand the content side of our faith, and God uses that content to raise our belief in him. Clark Pinnock writes, "The Spirit creates certitude in the heart on the basis of good and sufficient evidence. . . . Faith . . . is man's response to the Word of God, the good news, as the Spirit attests the Christ event past and the Christ presence now."[3]

A Father's Letter

Recently I read about an American soldier who became separated from a daughter he fathered during the Vietnam war. The mother, a Vietnamese woman, had died shortly after the daughter's birth, and the father had fled the country as the Viet Cong overtook Saigon. He had lost all hope of ever seeing his daughter again when, much to his surprise, he saw her in a photograph, along with other Vietnamese children, in a national magazine. The girl, now a teenager, looked just like him. So he wrote to her and, after two years of diplomatic negotiating, they were reunited.

I wondered what it must have been like the first time the girl received a letter from her father. Imagine the love, affection, and reassurance he must have poured into it and the many letters that followed. And think of what went through her mind. She had known of his existence for years, but now she began learning about the kind of person he was. With each new letter from the United States she learned more about her father.

I suspect she memorized facts about her father ("He's six feet tall, blue eyes, an engineer") and, if asked, I expect she could rattle off every fact that she could glean from the letters. I imagine she experienced his love and concern for her through his words, and so—in a small way—she came to know him.

Of course, for the girl to experience her father's love personally she had actually to meet him. The letters sustained her until she came to America, but what she got from the letters could never be compared to her later personal acquaintance with her father.

Scripture is analogous to the father's letters. The Bible is like a series of letters from a heavenly Father to his children, telling us how much he loves us and of his goal that we should know him personally through his Son, Jesus Christ. We are like orphans living in a far-off land, rejected by all and without hope—except for the slim possibility of being contacted by our father and rescued from captivity. But there is nothing we can do to contact him; *he* must find *us,* communicate with us, and save us. We are totally dependent on him.

If the Bible is God's letter, then the Holy Spirit is the postal carrier who delivers it to us. That is why the ministry of the Holy Spirit is so important; he is the key to our experiencing a personal relationship with God as we read Scripture, illuminating the words of the Bible and bringing us into contact with their Author. The Spirit's inspiration is also the key to how the Bible was written. Let's look at that topic next.

7

The Inspired Word

Paul says in 2 Timothy 3:16–17, "All Scripture is God-breathed and is useful for teaching, rebuking, correcting and training in righteousness, so that the man of God may be thoroughly equipped for every good work."[1] When theologians say the Bible was given by *inspiration,* they mean it is "God-breathed."

The Bible is not merely *inspiring* (like Dante or Shakespeare), it is *inspired*. The very words of the Old and New Testaments are the product of divine activity, God working through men who cooperate with him. Peter says, "Above all, you must understand that no prophecy of Scripture came about by the prophet's own interpretation. For prophecy never had its origin in the will of man but men spoke from God as they were carried along by the Holy Spirit" (2 Pet. 1:20–21).

The Nature of Inspiration

When Paul says that "all Scripture is God-breathed," he does not mean that God audibly dictated each word to the various writers. In fact the term "inspiration" does not imply anything about the *manner* in which God "breathed out" the various words that became

Scripture. God spoke to the prophets and to the writers of Scripture in many ways (Heb. 1:1). He spoke to them in audible voices, in inaudible voices in their minds, in dreams and visions, and so on. He led them to use historical research to write Scripture (Luke 1:1–4). In Paul's case the Spirit of God even led him to use truth contained in the writings of secular poets of the day (Acts 17:28).[2]

The biblical doctrine of inspiration teaches us that the words of Scripture are "the very words of God" (Rom. 3:2), but it does not limit the manner in which these words were given to the individual authors. One of my favorite definitions of inspiration has been formulated by Charles C. Ryrie: "God superintended the human authors of the Bible so that they composed and recorded without error His message to mankind in the words of their original writings."[3]

Because God used men to write his words, each book bears the personality of both its human and its divine author. Both the Holy Spirit *and* human beings were involved in writing Scripture. Nevertheless, the critical element was the Holy Spirit; his presence ensured that what was written was wholly true—true in the ways of God's choosing, if not always in the ways acceptable to modern men and women.

Many people find it difficult to accept the whole Bible as the word of God. Some believe parts of the Bible are in error; they reserve the right to pick and choose only those passages they agree with. Others believe the Bible "contains" the word of God and that it is the word of God only to the extent that we experience God in reading it. But if we reject the Bible's divine inspiration we miss out on the primary source of God's revelation. The Bible ceases to be a power point and instead becomes a doubting point in which individual passages are accepted or rejected on the basis of literary, historical, or philosophical criteria.[4]

For centuries Christian theologians have used several terms to summarize the high view of biblical inspiration. Some of these terms were used to combat false teachers who were undermining the authority of the Bible. Others were drawn directly from Scripture itself. However, though a few of the terms may not be found in

Scripture, each captures a critical characteristic of the Bible. It is important that we are familiar with the truth that each term represents, for they all motivate us to submit to Scripture as God's word:[5]

1. *Infallible*. This means Scripture will never deceive us, never lead us astray. It is wholly trustworthy and wholly reliable. It contains no mistakes and is incapable of error. God cannot lie (Titus 1:2), so his word will not mislead us.

It is important to remember that Scripture is infallible in its intended assertions. For example, when it refers to Moses parting the Red Sea we understand that this was a real event in history. When it says that God loves us, we assume that this is God's true intention. Discerning God's intention helps resolve apparent problems. For example, in order to illustrate a spiritual truth about faith, Jesus referred to the mustard seed as the smallest of seeds (Matt. 13:31–32). We know that in fact the mustard seed is not the smallest of all seeds. But Jesus' *intention* in this parable was not to teach botany. Still, the mustard seed was the smallest agricultural seed known to farmers at that time, and that was all that his words implied.

Meteorologists use speech in the same fashion today when they make statements like "The sun will rise at exactly 6:15." We know that the sun does not "rise"; the earth's rotation creates an illusion of it rising. When meteorologists speak of the sun "rising," their intention is to tell us when we will first see it; what they say may be scientifically inaccurate yet idiomatically correct.

2. *Inerrant*. The Bible is also wholly true. What the Bible says, God says. The idea of inerrancy comes from the attitude that Christ had toward Scripture, which was one of total trust, and it comes from Scripture itself: "I, the Lord, speak the truth; I declare what is right" (Isa. 45:19; see also Prov. 30:5–6). This is not to say that an error contained in Scripture would destroy belief in Christ's deity, the resurrection, or any other cardinal truth of Christianity. However, it would undermine our *confidence* that the Bible is wholly true, a trustworthy authority and guide in all matters of faith and practice.

In recent years much controversy has surrounded the idea of biblical inerrancy. I am not suggesting here that belief in inerrancy is necessary for salvation. Furthermore, inerrancy is not the basis for church membership or fellowship. But biblical inerrancy removes all doubt surrounding the reliability and authority of the Bible in all matters of faith and practice. If Jesus Christ is Lord, then we must hold the same high view of Scripture as he did. He commanded us to believe and obey the Bible and in this way to be his obedient and faithful disciples.

3. *Plenary.* Plenary inspiration means the Bible is fully inspired in all its parts. Romans 15:4 says, "For everything that was written in the past was written to teach us, so that through endurance and the encouragement of the Scriptures we might have hope." This means all of Scripture is inspired. This was a significant point for Carol and me when we first started reading the Bible. For a while we were fearful of finding an unbelievable passage, a portion of Scripture that was obviously fabricated and full of error. We reasoned that if one part were in error the whole document could be suspect.

4. *Verbal.* Inspiration extends to the words of Scripture themselves, and not only to the ideas contained in Scripture. Clark Pinnock writes, "If inspiration were not verbal, it would be irrelevant," because the message can only be conveyed by words. Therefore, God must control the words used. Of course the original words were Greek, Hebrew, or Aramaic, and we read English. But because their meaning can be translated accurately, an honest translation can convey the same truth.

5. *Confluent.* This means the Bible is both the words of men and the word of God. It has dual authorship. Though I mentioned this above, it warrants repeating: God did not merely dictate the Bible to writer-secretaries, as though human authors had no more of a part in producing Scripture than does the word processor on which I write this book. No, the Bible is the word of God spoken through human writers, and as such it bears the marks of humanity: God's truth is communicated in the authors' unique language and

culture. This dynamic is captured in 2 Samuel 23:2: "The Spirit of the Lord spoke through me; his word was on my tongue" (see also 1 Cor. 2:6–11; 2 Pet. 1:19–21).

The divine and human aspects of Scripture cannot be separated. We have no right to stand in judgment upon Scripture, separating and discarding supposedly human "myth" from divine "truth." (This holds true as long as we do not think the Bible is saying something it does not intend to say.) God has spoken through the human authors, used their unique personalities, and their words are the word of God.

6. *Clear.* The Bible is clear enough for us to read and understand it. Psalm 119:105 says, "Your word is a lamp to my feet and a light for my path." This does not mean *every* passage in the Bible is easy to understand (2 Pet. 3:16), but there is enough clarity to live by.[6] The Bible is written for ordinary believers, not just for "experts." In the fourth century Augustine said, "In the clear passages of Scripture everything is found that pertains to faith and life."

7. *Sufficient.* Clark Pinnock says that "to confess sufficiency and clarity is just to affirm that Scripture contains *enough light* to save sinners and direct the church." In 2 Timothy 3:15 Paul reminds Timothy that the Scriptures "are able to make you wise for salvation through faith in Christ Jesus." This is not to say that the Bible exhausts all possible or even all actual revelation (John 21:25) or that it reveals everything that can be known about God (1 Cor. 13:12). But it does mean that no modern revelations from God are to be placed on a level equal to Scripture in authority. In other words, any source of "revelation" that contradicts or exalts itself above Scripture is to be rejected (Deut. 13:1–5; Gal. 1:8–9).

If the Scriptures lacked clarity and sufficiency, we would require other authoritative sources of revelation to complement and enlighten them. One source of extrabiblical "revelation" is *ideology.* In the 1920s and 1930s many "German Christians" attempted to accommodate the message of faith to the values and ideals of modern culture—in this instance, to the ideology of national socialism.

National socialism was based on the philosophy of evolution and the belief that the Aryan race is the "fittest." Following this evil ideology, the theologian Alfred Rosenberg accused Paul of corrupting the teaching of Jesus: "Our Pauline churches are not Christian but consciously or unconsciously a gigantic falsification of the message of Jesus."[7] Rosenberg was unwilling to accept the "Jewish" Gospels of Matthew and Luke or any of Paul's Letters. In addition to rejecting some passages of Scripture, some "German Christians" rewrote Scripture to make it conform to Nazi ideology.[8] In the end, these "German Christians" fell prey to placing ideology over Scripture; the results were disastrous. (It should be noted that not all German Christians yielded to this heresy.)

Another source of extrabiblical "revelation" is *tradition*. The use of tradition, especially the writings of great theologians and leaders from the early church, appears on the surface to be a valid way of resolving disagreements over the interpretation of Scripture. But "tradition" includes a vast body of literature; just *who* determines which tradition is *the* authoritative tradition? The problem of biblical interpretation is only compounded when tradition is given equal authority with Scripture. However, it should be noted that tradition can be useful in *confirming* and *illuminating* the teaching of Scripture. The majority of tradition, especially the creeds from the great ecumenical councils of the first five centuries, are concise statements that reflect core biblical truths.

Finally, some people believe *mystical experience* or *private revelation* is equal to or superior to Scripture. This is dangerous, because "truth" that is determined by an inner revelation lies outside the scope of objective restraints. Under these conditions, subjectivity poses as Christianity. Personal experience and private revelation need the checks and guidance that only the Bible can provide. When personal revelation touches on fundamental issues of doctrine and morality, it is valid only if it conforms to biblical values. In 1977 God led me to begin praying for the sick. Over the next ten months I did not see anyone healed; during this period there were many times when I wanted to give up. But each time the Holy Spirit chastened me—through personal revelation in which I sensed him speaking—commanding me to keep praying. I was confident that my experience was from God, because in Scripture the Lord and the disciples prayed for the sick. Long ago I chose Jesus as my model for the Christian life. So my purpose in praying for the sick was merely to fulfill Scripture, not add to it.

Saying private revelation cannot be normative over the Bible does not mean all private revelation is false. "To deny the possibility of private revelation," Clark Pinnock writes, "would be to imply that God is now silent."[9] The purpose of Scripture is to bring us into union with Christ and into relationship with his Father. If out of fear of devaluing Scripture we cast a shadow over all Christian experience, we reduce Christianity to a set of rules and miss out on the joy of knowing the living God. (I will say more about how God speaks to us in Chapter 10.)

8. *Efficacy.* Finally, Scripture is effective in bringing people to a personal relationship with Christ. The word of God generates eternal life. Peter says, "For you have been born again, not of perishable seed, but of imperishable, through the living and enduring word of God" (1 Pet. 1:23). Through the power of the Holy Spirit, the word of God also creates saving faith. It overcomes unbelief and promotes salvation (Rom. 10:17). Further, it judges our hearts. "For the word of God is living and active. Sharper than any double-edged sword, it penetrates even to dividing soul and spirit, joints and marrow; it judges the thoughts and attitudes of the heart" (Heb. 4:12). This passage highlights the dynamic word of God, a living power that judges as an all-seeing eye, penetrating a person's innermost being.

Knowing about Scripture isn't the same as knowing Scripture, which is the topic of the rest of this section.

8

A Passion for God's Word

I have devoted considerable space to describing biblical inspiration and authority in order to establish one point: We need the Bible because it is God's authoritative voice, expressing his claims on all men and women. This truth should put an insatiable hunger for God's word in our hearts and minds.

Yet much of the time we approach Scripture as we do *medication* when we are sick. We have a need when wounded or hurting—so we go for comfort, counsel, hope. We know it is good for us, so we read it; but frequently it is a joyless chore. And like most medicine, sometimes it does not taste very good. It is, after all, a mirror of the sin that may be in our lives. This makes it easy to forget to take our daily dose, especially when our needs are not too pressing.

We also read Scripture as *nourishment,* for the wisdom and perspective that helps us live and grow. Through it we learn who we are and where we are going. We keep coming back more out of habit than out of conviction, only occasionally skipping a meal. I believe most Christians with disciplined devotional lives have a nutritional motivation to reading the Bible; they know it is good for them.

Now do not misunderstand me. Whatever our motivation for reading Scripture, when we spend time with God in his word it is to our benefit. Meditating on God's word for healing and nourishment are adequate (and scriptural) reasons for reading. But God has a better way, fueled by a more pure motive, for us. He wants us to develop a *passion* for Scripture that makes our desire for thick Texas steaks or succulent New England lobsters pale in comparison.

Recently I took a close look at my own heart, and I had to admit that I had more of a "take your medicine" mentality than a deep and joyful spiritual hunger for the Bible. So I asked God to instill in me again a hunger for his word. "Lord," I prayed—and continue praying—"give me a passion for you and for your word. Place in me a hunger that can only be satisfied by you."

My prayers paid off. My devotional life came alive; the word of God became my delight once again, much as it was when I first became a Christian. Now I can hardly put the Bible down at the end of my devotional time. Scripture study and prayer are the highest priorities of my life. On the rare occasions that I miss my devotions I struggle more with unsatisfied spiritual hunger than with the guilt.

Wrong Attitudes

I have observed two attitudes toward Scripture that inhibit many Christians from allowing the Bible to have full authority in their lives.

The first is the "leave it to the experts" mentality, where people abdicate personal responsibility for knowing God in Scripture. Modern theologians and pastors have unwittingly contributed to this problem. Armed with the latest discoveries in linguistics, anthropology, psychology, sociology, and history, they leave most laypeople with the impression that interpreting the Bible is too complex an operation for the ordinary person.

The second attitude runs counter to the first. It is the "me and my Bible" mentality: a subjective, feeling-oriented approach that resists others' insights. In many instances Christians use the Bible to shield themselves from authority in their lives, especially from pastors and more mature Christians. But the Bible teaches that we are an interdependent people, and the wisdom and understanding of pastoral leaders are vital elements of the Christian life.

Right Attitudes

How do we resolve the tension between relying too much on the experts, on the one hand, and relying too much on ourselves, on the other?

When I stick to the following principles I usually meet God in Scripture study:

1. *Read to learn from God.* This includes both devotional reading as well as study. Devotional reading involves meditating and praying over Scripture. Ponder. Think. Stop and ask God what he is saying to *you*. Remember Jesus' words: "Take my yoke upon you and learn from me" (Matt. 11:29). I am convinced that most Christians do not spend enough time reading Scripture devotionally. When Bible reading is neglected in favor of Bible study only, we miss out on the devotional benefits of the word of God.

2. *Read to obey.* If we learn about God but never act on what we learn, we risk coming under Jesus' judgment of the Pharisees. He said, "they do not practice what they preach" (Matt. 23:3). James comes straight to the point for Christians when he writes,

> Do not merely listen to the word, and so deceive yourselves. Do
> what it says. Anyone who listens to the word but does not do what
> it says is like a man who looks at his face in a mirror and, after
> looking at himself, goes away and immediately forgets what he
> looks like. But the man who looks intently into the perfect law that
> gives freedom, and continues to do this, not forgetting what he has
> heard, but doing it—he will be blessed in what he does. (James
> 1:22–25)

Scripture is a mirror of reality, revealing masks that cover our faces and telling us how to remove them. How can we know what God expects of us if we do not know his will? And of what benefit is his will if we do not act on it?

3. *Read to share with others.* If we read the Bible only for ourselves, we miss out on one of the key dynamics of the word of God.

The Lord gives us his light so that we may show the way to others. Many times I experience an unexpected blessing when I share from God's word with others. My understanding deepens, and the word of God comes alive even more.

Psalm 119, a devotional meditation on the word of God, uses several analogies to describe the Bible's beneficial qualities. Verse 98 says, "Your commands make me wiser than my enemies." We do not need a doctorate in theology to participate in the wisdom of Scripture.

"How sweet are your words to my taste," says verse 103, "sweeter than honey to my mouth!" We do not have to be nutritionists to appreciate the sweetness of honey! The sweetness of Scripture is even better, if only we take the time to read and obey it.

Verse 127 says, "I love your commands more than gold, more than pure gold . . ." We do not have to be experts in precious metals to appreciate the value of God's word.

Verse 130 says, "The unfolding of your words gives light; it gives understanding to the simple." We do not have to be electricians or physicists to benefit from light. Simply living under Scripture, reading and submitting to it, is like turning on a light in a room. It displaces the darkness.

Holding the right attitudes may motivate us to read Scripture, but we need more understanding to intrepret it accurately. That is the topic of the next chapter.

9

Interpreting God's Word

We all interpret Scripture. That is, we make assessments of what a passage means and draw conclusions about how it applies to our lives. As Gordon Fee and Douglas Stuart say, "The most important ingredient one brings to that task [of interpretation] is enlightened common sense. The test of good interpretation is that it makes good sense of the text."[1]

Basics of Interpretation

I have often heard it said, "The plain thing is the main thing, and the main thing is the plain thing." The aim of interpretation is to know the plain meaning of a text, and what is obvious and straight-forward in the text is the most significant point for the reader to grasp. With just a few simple skills, some basic resources, and a willingness to ask questions, anyone can study the Bible and interpret it with reasonable accuracy. The following steps are helpful for do-it-yourself Bible study:

1. *Get prepared.* Though we do not have to be scholars to study the Bible, scholars do provide tools that make our job much easier. I recommend keeping on hand two or three different translations of the Bible,[2] a standard Bible handbook, and a good concordance. I

also find study Bibles quite helpful. And do not forget the most overlooked tool of all: a good Bible dictionary. All of these are available at your local Christian bookstore.[3]

2. *Observe.* After I decide on a passage of Scripture to study, I read it and passages around it to discover its main thought and context. Reading it aloud two or three times often gives me a better feel for the passage. When I see an emerging theme, I stop and write it down. And reading different translations usually sheds new insights on the passage I am studying. I ask myself, "What are the main points that the author is making?" and then attempt to express them in my own words.

The plain meaning of any text is the original, intended meaning of the author. What we are trying to do is hear the text as the original author intended. This is not always easy to accomplish. As we have seen, the Bible is at the same time the word of God and the words of men; it was written within a historical context that we must understand if we are to grasp the original intent of the authors. They wrote in different cultures, in different languages, thousands of years ago. To understand what the authors intended their readers to understand requires careful reading and, in some instances, outside help.

A key principle to remember at this stage is that the primary interpreter of Scripture is Scripture itself. One maxim that I have found helpful when I encounter a difficult verse or passage is this: "Keep reading." Read one scripture in the light of all the rest.

3. *Search for facts.* Answer these five questions about the passage:

- Who? (*Persons*) Who is the author? To whom is he writing? About whom is he writing? What do you know about these people?
- What? (*Content*) What is the subject at hand? What are the circumstances that have influenced the author? What exactly does the author mean by certain statements?
- Where? (*Place*) Where was the writer when he wrote? Which part of the world is it being written for? How

would one describe the religious, political, and economic circumstances of that city or region of the world?

- When? (*Time*) Was the passage written before Christ's first coming or shortly after his death? Or toward the end of the first century?
- Why? (*Motive*) Why is the author writing about this particular topic? Why does he want us to do or believe certain things?

These questions are easily answered with a good study Bible or Bible handbook.

4. *Interpret the meaning.* Next I go through the text and circle or write down repeated words or phrases. Usually I see a pattern that leads to a rough outline of the passage.

When a key word emerges, I study it in greater detail. If I am unsure about its meaning, I look it up in a dictionary. Next, I look it up in a concordance and read how it is used in other passages. This is called cross-referencing. Finally, I look the word up in one of my reference books.

At this point I observe principles, or universal truths, emerging from the passage. These principles were as true in biblical times as they are today, and they are the jewels that make my study worthwhile.

5. *Apply.* Scripture study is valid only if we put into action what God shows us. Throughout the entire process of Scripture study I pray, again and again, "God, show me your truth, and show me how to live it and give it to others." This means cultivating an attitude of listening to God and an openness to doing what he says.

John White suggests we keep in mind questions like these[4] as we apply Scripture to our lives:

- Is there a *warning* for me here?
- Is there a *promise* I can claim?
- Is there an *example* for me to follow?
- Are there *commands* I must obey?
- Is there a *sin* I must avoid or confess?

- Is there some *encouragement* I can take to heart?
- Is there some new *lesson* about God I can thank him for?
- Are there words of *praise* I can echo?
- Is there an *experience* described that has been true of me?

Almost without exception, when God shows me a universal truth, he provides an opportunity to integrate it into my life and share it with others. That is what is so wonderful about Scripture study!

Conservators

Earlier in Part III, I compared the Bible with an American GI's letters to his long-lost Vietnamese daughter. For two years she received letters while he tried to get her released from Vietnam. I imagine that she saved every letter he sent. They were, without question, the most precious objects she owned. We are called to conserve the Bible in a similar way, for in so doing we guard God's truth and maintain our relationship with him.

The great leaders of the church have always been conservators of God's word. For example, Augustine wrote, "Do not follow my writings as Holy Scripture. When you find in Holy Scripture anything you did not believe before, believe it without doubt; but in my writings, you should hold nothing for certain."[5] Luther, the great Reformer, said,

> We must make a great difference between God's Word and the word
> of man. A man's word is a little sound, that flies into the air, and
> soon vanishes; but the Word of God is greater than heaven and
> earth, yea, greater than death and hell, for it forms part of the
> power of God, and endures everlastingly.[6]

Communicators

Of course the Vietnamese girl also probably told everyone she came into contact with about her father. Can you not see her, reading sections from the letters to friends and strangers, showing them his picture, describing in detail what she knew about his home and occupation? Nobody could meet her without learning something about her father, because the letters were lifelines to a living relationship.

Again, the analogy to the Christian and the Bible is striking. We are called to be communicators as well as conservators of God's word. I preach the gospel, teach, worship, feed the poor, house the homeless, pray for the sick, prophesy, and so on, because the Bible says that is what lovers of God do!

To do anything less, to fail to combine the word of God with the works of the Spirit, is to hold something less than a high view of Scripture. Jesus said, "If anyone loves me, he will obey my teaching. My Father will love him, and we will come to him and make our home with him. He who does not love me will not obey my teaching" (John 14:23–24).

The Bible is unlike any other book. It is a collection of incredible love letters from God, telling us about our relationship with him. Small wonder that we are called to be men and women of "The Book," meditating daily on God's word and allowing it to transform our minds, hearts, souls, and actions.

The Bible teaches that God communicates with us in many ways. Hearing God's voice is the topic we will explore in the next chapter.

10

Hearing God's Word

David Watson, in his outstanding book *Called & Committed*, writes, "If every word that God speaks is vital for us, how does God speak today? How can we both hear and understand his word rightly?"[1] We have already seen that God reveals himself to us through his Son, Jesus Christ, who is referred to in Scripture as the Word of God (John 1:1, 14, 18). In him we see the Father:[2]

> In the past God spoke to our forefathers through the prophets at many times and in various ways, but in these last days he has spoken to us by his Son, whom he appointed heir of all things, and through whom he made the universe. The Son is the radiance of God's glory and the exact representation of his being. (Heb. 1:1–3)

We know God most perfectly, then, by knowing his Son. Jesus is the highest and most perfect revelation of God.

Scripture

We have seen that the Bible is also called the word of God, for it is the written record that reveals Jesus, who is the incarnate Word of God. Through it we receive an accurate historical record and authentic interpretation of Jesus' acts, so there can be no misunderstanding about who he is. The Bible is the principle source from which we learn about God.

Though the Old and New Testaments are our final court of appeal in matters pertaining to faith and practice, they are not the only way in which God speaks to us. In fact the Bible teaches that God communicates with us in a variety of ways. Rejecting these other means of revelation shuts off important avenues through which God speaks to us. And it means a loss of opportunity for spiritual growth and service.

God speaks to all men and women through creation, through our consciences, and through his continuing providence. But it does not end there. In the Old and New Testaments we see God speaking to his children in dramatic, sometimes startling ways: dreams and visions, inner impressions, angels, tongues and interpretations, words of wisdom, words of knowledge, discernment of spirits, preaching, teaching, witnessing, prophesying, circumstances, and even personal appearances.

God continued to speak to Christians through dreams, visions, prophetic utterances, and so on, even after Jesus ascended to the Father. Stephen, Philip, Ananias, Cornelius, Agabus, Judas and Silas, and Philip's four daughters experienced angelic visitations, dreams, and visions (Acts 7:54–60; 8:26–40; 10:3–8; Acts 11:28; 21:10–11; 15:32; 21:9). Philip's experience with the Ethiopian eunuch in Acts 8 is truly remarkable. It includes an angelic visitation, the Holy Spirit speaking directly to him, and the Spirit bodily transporting him away to Azotus.

Danger

The idea that God can and does speak to us in such ways frightens some Christians, because it involves subjective experience. They readily accept preaching, teaching, and witnessing as authentic ways God speaks to us, for they are so clearly rooted in Scripture. But some of the other means of communication are not as easy to verify.

For example, how reliable is guidance from an angelic visitation or prophecy?

Some Christians believe that more subjective expressions of God's communication open the door to emotional or, far more significantly, satanic deception. Fearing the worst, they retreat to the position that the Bible is the *sole* source of revelation today. (Their position is not that God *could not* speak today in these ways, but that he has chosen not to.)

But this is actually an unbiblical position! The Bible clearly teaches that we should expect God to speak to us in a variety of ways. Two texts from Luke explicitly encourage us to expect revelation from the Holy Spirit:

> [Jesus said,] "When you are brought before synagogues, rulers and authorities, do not worry about how you will defend yourselves or what you will say, for the Holy Spirit will teach you at that time what you should say." (Luke 12:11–12)
>
> [Jesus said,] "But make up your mind not to worry beforehand how you will defend yourselves. For I will give you words and wisdom that none of your adversaries will be able to resist or contradict." (Luke 21:14–15)

Guidelines

Still, it is proper to seek biblical guidelines regarding direct revelation. What safeguards does Scripture provide to ensure that we are not led astray, especially by "prophetic" words?

1. *Personal words should glorify the Word of God, Jesus Christ.* The Holy Spirit's primary mission is to bring glory to the Son (John 16:14), so any prophecy, dream, or vision should point us toward Jesus.

2. *They should conform to the word of God, the Bible.* Paul says that elders must "encourage others by sound doctrine and refute those who oppose it" (Titus 1:9). The content of extrabiblical revelation should always be in accordance with and submitted to Scripture.

3. *If a person delivers a word, he or she should be of sound moral character and submitted to the lordship of Jesus* (Matt. 7:15–20). A good test of mature character is to see if the messenger is submitted to pastoral oversight. Independent, unteachable, and self-proclaimed "prophets" are dangerous.[3]

4. *A person delivering prophecies should be willing to have his or her words tested* (1 Cor. 14:29–32). Pastoral oversight tests prophetic ministry and guides its recipients in appropriate responses. Complaints or questions about specific prophetic ministry should be thoroughly investigated and brought to clear resolution by responsible pastors.

5. *Prophetic words should be given in the spirit of love* (James 3:17). Even a word of rebuke is to be given in the spirit of love. Information about individuals that is negative or may be embarrassing should not be spoken publicly without first confronting the individual in private. In general, prophetic gifting should not be used for controlling purposes, and should be overseen to ensure that believers' personal responsibility and authority for their own lives are not undermined, and so that pastoral authority over a church is not undermined.

6. *Prophecy should not be used to establish doctrine or practice without clear biblical support* (1 Tim. 6:3). Some experiences and "revelations" are outside the scope of both Scripture and of everyday experience and therefore should not be looked to as authoritative truth.

7. *No one should make major decisions based on personal prophetic words alone* (1 Cor. 14:29–32). Personal prophetic words should be weighed by elders, pastors, and other prophetic people, as well as the person who is receiving the word. Personal words should be given in a way and in a setting that allows for this to happen. For example, the prophet Agabus warned Paul that if he went to Jerusalem he would be arrested, and the other disciples pleaded with him not to go. Paul accepted the prophetic word but still went on to Jerusalem, where he was later arrested. He accepted the revelation of his coming suffering, but he rejected the disciples' application—that he therefore should not go (Acts 21:10–14).

8. *If a prophetic word predicts future events, it should be fulfilled.* If God has truly spoken, the events will happen. If the predicted events do not happen, either God has not spoken (Deut. 18:21–22) or unspoken conditions of the prophecy were not fulfilled (Jonah; Jer. 18:7–10).

9. *Many if not most personal prophetic words given today are conditional, and as such are invitations, not certainties* (Jer. 18:7–10). We must continue to seek God for the promised blessings to come to pass.

The key to hearing God's word is knowing his voice (John 10:3), and to know God's voice we must know the Father. That is the topic of Part IV.

PART IV

Seeking the Father

II

Seeking the Father's Face

In August 1987 I had a life-changing experience. It started innocently enough. I was having lunch with Michael and Rosemary Green at a restaurant near Fuller Seminary in Pasadena, California. Michael, who is a professor at Regent College in Vancouver, British Columbia, was teaching a two-week course on personal evangelism at Fuller. We were taking advantage of their being near my home to develop our relationship. Up to that time we were only acquaintances.

After lunch our conversation drifted toward my background. The Greens wanted to know more about me. Soon I was talking about my childhood and early adulthood. Normally I avoid giving intimate details about my life, but I felt comfortable and safe with the Greens. In fact I felt so comfortable that I trapped them into listening to me for over an hour!

At the time I was in a melancholy mood, struggling with personal and ministry challenges. I was still suffering physically after an angina attack I'd had in June 1986; the growing Vineyard church movement needed my immediate care and energy; and at Fuller Seminary the controversy surrounding a course I had helped teach resulted in criticism that both surprised and disappointed me.

While I was still talking, Rosemary leaned forward, looked me square in the eyes, and said, "You've been hurt and disappointed by many male authority figures in your life, beginning with your father, haven't you?" Her words contained more than the weight of mere observation. They seemed anointed by God with supernatural wisdom, insight, and power. She went on to say that she had a suspicion that I had not adequately dealt with my disappointments, and that they had taken a spiritual and emotional toll on my life.

In an instant a casual lunch with new friends was transformed into an encounter with the living God. Michael and Rosemary suggested that we return to their apartment for prayer. I agreed.

Rejection

At the apartment, as we talked, I realized that beginning in childhood I had experienced rejection and abandonment from a succession of father and authority figures. The most significant rejection occurred on February 25, 1934—the day of my birth. I had barely emerged from my mother's womb when my father abandoned both mom and me. This, along with the fact that I had no brothers or sisters, explains why I was so withdrawn as a child, spending long hours alone, practicing my musical instruments. Eventually my mom remarried, but my stepfather—a good man—never filled the void left by my father.

The hurt and feelings of rejection caused by my absent father's departure remained buried deep in my heart, like an infected wound. Matters were not helped when I finally met my natural father. I was in my early twenties, and I hoped that a meaningful reunion would recover what I had missed out on in childhood—a loving relationship with my dad. But once again I was to be disappointed. Early in our conversation he revealed himself with the question, "Can you hold your liquor like your old man?" There was nothing there but more pain.

When I became a Christian I gained a true Friend—one to whom I could talk about anything and from whom I could receive direction for everything. I also gained a mediator who opened the door to a relationship with my heavenly Father. But while a brotherly relationship with Jesus came naturally, a relationship with the Father did not come nearly as easily. My experience with my natural father created a barrier to trusting my heavenly Father. How could I be sure that he, too, would not abandon me? So, for much of my Christian life I unconsciously avoided thinking of God as Father.

It did not help that many of my *Christian* mentors—pastors, professors, supervisors—also abandoned me when I needed them most. Or at least I *perceived* them as abandoning me. But it is not surprising that I perceived them this way. I placed such high expectations on our relationships that inevitably they *had* to fail me. None of them were God, and none of them could replace the father I never had. Only my heavenly Father could meet my expectations, and I was not on speaking terms with him! (Or at least I did not *feel* as though I was.)

Prayer

Rosemary very lovingly and skillfully (and with great gifting from the Holy Spirit) ministered to me, with Michael looking on and praying quietly. I found myself opening up to them. I had been a Christian for twenty-five years and a pastor for eighteen, yet in those few minutes of prayer I experienced God's fatherly love more than I had in my entire Christian life.

I admitted to God that my father and the others who had let me down had inflicted great hurt and caused great confusion in my life. (Most of the harm was unintentional on their part, but nevertheless it was real to me.) I had to release all of these disappointments, especially that of not having known my natural father, and I had to ask forgiveness for any bitterness and anger that I held toward God. Then I experienced his forgiveness and love, and I affirmed my relationship with him as my Father.

In retrospect, I see that without the Holy Spirit I was incapable of understanding the depth of my hurt, of extending forgiveness to my natural father, and of fully experiencing my heavenly Father's love. Before that time I knew *intellectually* about the Father—that he is the First Person of the Trinity, that Jesus came to reveal him to us, and that I had access to him. And, to some degree, I knew the Father *spiritually*. But after I prayed with Rosemary and Michael I knew him with greater depth and intimacy. Since that time I have experienced a new kind of freedom and access to God—freedom and access that I never had before.

12

One God, Three Persons

Where do we get this notion of calling God our Father? Up until now I have been talking about the Father, and about Jesus, and about the Holy Spirit. Before we go on let us pause for a while to try to understand what the Bible says about these three Persons and how they together constitute one God.

A clear knowledge of the Trinity only comes from Christian revelation. The concept of the Trinity is difficult to understand and can never be understood fully; finite human beings need a good dose of humility when approaching the infinite God of the Bible. This does not mean we know *nothing* about God. He has revealed enough of himself for us to know him personally, though we will never exhaust our knowledge of him.

The term "Trinity" is not found in the Bible, but the concept of a triune God is. Scripture teaches that the Father is God (Matt. 11:25), the Son is God (Rom. 9:5), and the Holy Spirit is God (Acts 5:3, 4).

Simply stated, the Trinity is Tri-unity: three Persons in one God. The Christian belief that there is only one God, which is called monotheism, is rooted in the Hebrew Old Testament. Deuteronomy 6:4 says, "Hear, O Israel: The Lord our God, the Lord is one."

This proclamation, known as the Shema, has always been Israel's great confession. It was particularly significant to the ancient Israelites, who were surrounded by a multiplicity of local "gods." Throughout their history the Jews occasionally drifted into the worship of these false gods, a sin for which God severely disciplined them throughout the Old Testament.[1] Jesus himself affirmed the Shema in Mark 12:29.

One God

Saying that God is one means he is one in essence, in nature. All three Persons—Father, Son, and Spirit—partake of the same infinite, uncreated being—not just the same *kind* of being, but the same being itself. There are no divisions, no parts of God. So there are not three gods, because all three Persons share the same essence.[2]

Saying God is one also means that the three Persons are always in perfect agreement and harmony. The three Persons agree in mind, will, and character in all things. In John 8:28 Jesus says, "I do nothing on my own but speak just what the Father has taught me."

Three Persons

The doctrine of the Trinity is not developed extensively in the Old Testament, though there are shadows of it from the beginning. Genesis 1:1–3 says, "In the beginning God created the heavens and the earth. Now the earth was formless and empty, darkness was over the surface of the deep, and *the Spirit of God* was hovering over the waters. And God said, 'Let there be light,' and there was light." The Spirit of God is mentioned in Genesis 1:2, and Christ—who is called "the Word" in the first chapter of John's Gospel—may be alluded to in verse 3. Later in Genesis 1:26 the writer uses the plural pronoun when referring to God: "Let *us* make man in *our* image, in *our* likeness . . ."[3]

Someone might say that there really are not three distinct Persons in the Trinity, but one God appearing at different times and places in three different forms. Sometimes God appears as the

Father, at other times as the Son, and still at other times the Holy Spirit. Yet the conversations and prayers that occur between the members of the Godhead demonstrate that there *are* three distinct Persons who are all God. For example, John 17 is the high-priestly prayer of the Son to the Father who is listening to the Son at that moment. Romans 8:26 and 8:34 teach us that both the Spirit and the Son are presently praying to the Father for the saints.

The Trinity is most explicitly referred to in the Great Commission, where Jesus commands us to baptize "in the name of the Father and of the Son and of the Holy Spirit" (Matt. 28:19). In 2 Corinthians 13:14 Paul says, "May the grace of the Lord Jesus Christ, and the love of God, and the fellowship of the Holy Spirit be with you all."[4]

Scripture describes order in the Trinity. There is submission and authority in the community of the Godhead. The Son submits to the Father (John 5:19), and the Spirit is sent to glorify the Son (John 15:26; 16:13–14). Jesus' willing submission to his Father demonstrates that not even God "does his own thing." When we are called on to submit to God, therefore, he is not asking us to do anything that he has not done himself!

There is also an emphasis on function in the Trinity. Although all works of God are done jointly by the three Persons, creation is primarily ascribed to the Father, redemption to the Son, and sanctification to the Holy Spirit.

The implications of the doctrine of the Trinity for Christians are many. The Trinity is the fullness of life, in eternal relationships and never-ending fellowship. God does not *need* men and women for fellowship, but he does *invite* us to enter into his fellowship. The Trinity also offers a basis for understanding unity and diversity in the universe; since there is diversity in God himself, might it not also be reflected in the universe?

Finally, the Trinity offers a model for family life and human relationships. The Father has always loved the Son, the Son glorifies the Father, the Spirit glorifies the Son, and so on. To learn what a truly loving family is, all we have to do is look to the Trinity.

13

Experiencing the Father's Blessing

Because I had seen my heavenly Father through the lens of my earthly experiences—many of them hurtful—I had a distorted view of his fatherhood. When I heard the words, "God is my Father," a variety of emotions and images came to my mind, some good and many bad. Mixed in with biblical images of forgiveness, protection, acceptance, and love were feelings of betrayal, failure, and absence. As a consequence, I related to the Father inadequately. Jesus was my brother; the Holy Spirit was my counselor; but the Father was an elusive, removed figure to be avoided. The less contact I had with him, the better the chance of avoiding disappointment when he did not come through. I was incapable of loving and trusting my heavenly Father as he intended me to, and I was missing out on what every human being needs: deeply personal fatherly love, protection, and care.

There are innumerable ways in which earthly fathers fail, creating obstacles to a loving relationship with our heavenly Father. I could spend the rest of this chapter—and many more books—exploring how fathers sin against their children. However, I believe that experiencing our heavenly Father's love is the best way to overcome past hurts, for through his love we *know* in the depth of our spirits that we are his adopted sons and daughters. Here are three aspects of the Father's love that, if taken to heart, can cure the worst cases of heartache and crushed spirits.[1]

1. *Faithfulness.* Everyone needs someone who believes in him or her, a person who is faithful, who can be counted on. God intended that fathers fill that role. A faithful father has two traits. First, he is a man of his word; he remembers what he promised and does his best to fulfill it. Second, a faithful father is always there when you need him most. Faithful fathers instill confidence and security in their children. If the children become Christians, they find it easy to trust God and believe his word, because they are accustomed to a father who has integrity and who is there to encourage them.[2]

Even the best dads are incapable of perfect faithfulness. They are finite and have only limited resources at their disposal. But our heavenly Father is without limits! Paul wrote, "God, who has called you into fellowship with his Son Jesus Christ our Lord, is faithful" (1 Cor. 1:9). The Father can be trusted to do what he promised, which includes helping us to complete running the race of the Christian life (Phil. 1:6; 1 Thess. 5:23–24).

Not only can we count on him, but he is always available—he is omnipresent, present everywhere at all times. He is, in Paul's words spoken to the Athenians at the Areopagus, "not far from each one of us" (Acts 17:27).

2. *Loving authority.* Paul warned fathers against exasperating and embittering their children, "or they [the children] will become discouraged" (Col. 3:21). When I pray for people with serious spiritual, emotional, or physical problems, I frequently uncover childhood abuse from their fathers. In recent years the media have acquainted us with obvious forms of abuse, especially beating and sexual molestation. But I suspect a more widespread problem is the breaking of children's spirits from criticism, rebuke, nagging, and cruel discipline.

The prescription for abusive authority is not doing away with authority. It is loving discipline. The writer of Hebrews says discipline from God is a sign that he loves us: "My son, do not make light of the Lord's discipline, and do not lose heart when he rebukes you, because the Lord disciplines those he loves, and he punishes everyone he accepts as a son" (Heb. 12:5–6, quoted from Prov. 3:11–12). The Greek word translated "discipline" in this passage is the same word Paul used in Ephesians 6:4, where he instructed fathers to train their children. If we have received loving discipline from our earthly fathers, it is much easier to receive it from our heavenly Father; if out of reaction to childhood abuse we run from God's discipline, we will miss out on "a harvest of righteousness and peace for those who have been trained by it" (Heb. 12:11).

3. *Generous blessing.* Gary Smalley and John Trent have written a book, *The Blessing,* in which they say parental blessing has a profound effect on present and future relationships. They define the parental blessing as "genuine acceptance" and say when it is missing people strive to find it, usually with disastrous results:

> Some people are driven toward workaholism as they search for the blessing they never received at home. Always striving for acceptance, they never feel satisfied that they are measuring up. Others get mired in withdrawal and apathy as they give up hope of ever truly being blessed. . . . For almost all children who miss out on their parents' blessing, at some level this lack of acceptance sets off a lifelong search.[3]

At the root of genuine acceptance is unconditional love. Unconditional love is based on a father's love for his children and not on their performance to please him. Paul says, "But because of his great love for us, God, who is rich in mercy, made us alive with Christ even when we were dead in transgressions—it is by grace you have been saved" (Eph. 2:4–5).

Smalley and Trent outline five basic parts to the blessing that communicate a significant aspect of a father's love for his children.[4]

The first is a *meaningful touch*—a compassionate arm around the shoulders, a hand of blessing on the heart, a reassuring pat on the arm. Intimate touches are gestures that say more than words; they are sacraments of fatherly affection, assuring us of his love and commitment. Our heavenly Father perfectly fulfills this part of the blessing; he freely offers the touch of his transforming love (1 Sam. 10:26). Our part is to receive his touch, to accept and experience the love of his Spirit resting in our hearts.

Second, for a blessing to have meaning it must be *articulated*. A loving father tells his children that he loves them, affirms them, believes in them. Our heavenly Father loves us so much that he has sent his Son to open communication lines with us. He even called Jesus "the Word of God" in John's Gospel (1:1–18).

A third aspect of fatherly blessing is *attaching high value* to the one being blessed. In the Sermon on the Mount Jesus said that our heavenly Father places immense value on us: "Look at the birds of the air; they do not sow or reap or store away in barns, and yet your heavenly Father feeds them. Are you not much more valuable than they?" (Matt. 6:26). Peter says that we, "like living stones, are being built into a spiritual house to be a holy priesthood . . ." (1 Pet. 2:5). God does not make junk, and he wants to tell us that! More important, he wants us to believe and experience the blessing of his approval.

Many people sense they have a destiny in life because their parents *picture a special future* for them, which Smalley and Trent define as the fourth part of blessing. Jesus blessed Simon Peter this way when, at the time of Peter's calling, he said, "Don't be afraid; from now on you will catch men" (Luke 5:10). Paul writes, "For we are God's workmanship, created in Christ Jesus *to do good works, which God prepared in advance for us to do*" (Eph. 2:10). Each one of us has a special future, works and blessings that have been prepared especially for us by our heavenly Father before the foundation of the world. No two futures are alike, because no two people are alike. And no one will be left out. Jesus said, "In my Father's house are many rooms; if it were not so, I would have told you. I am going there to prepare a place for you" (John 14:2).

The fifth part of a fatherly blessing is *an active commitment to fulfill the blessing.* At the heart of the cross was our heavenly Father's willingness to sacrifice his own Son to gain eternal life for us. Everything that God does is generous: his creation is rich in variety, beauty, and color; he cares for every detail of our lives; he lavishes his grace on us (Eph. 1:7–8). His blessing becomes a power point in our lives when we experience it by faith. Talking about the Fatherly blessing is not enough; we need to open our hearts up and receive it if we want to know his life-changing love.

14

The Parable of the Father's Love

Jesus revealed his Father's attitude toward us in the parable of the prodigal son. I prefer to call it "the parable of the Father's love,"[1] because it reminds me of how God the Father receives us when we turn to him:

"There was a man who had two sons. The younger one said to his father, 'Father, give me my share of the estate.' So he divided his property between them.

"Not long after that, the younger son got together all he had, set off for a distant country and there squandered his wealth in wild living. After he had spent everything, there was a severe famine in that whole country, and he began to be in need. So he went and hired himself out to a citizen of that country, who sent him to his fields to feed pigs. He longed to fill his stomach with the pods that the pigs were eating, but no one gave him anything.

"When he came to his senses, he said, 'How many of my father's hired men have food to spare, and here I am starving to death! I will set out and go back to my father and say to him: Father, I have sinned against heaven and against you. I am no longer worthy to be called your son; make me like one of your hired men.' So he got up and went to his father.

"But while he was still a long way off, his father saw him and was filled with compassion for him; he ran to his son, threw his arms around him and kissed him.

"The son said to him, 'Father, I have sinned against heaven and against you. I am no longer worthy to be called your son.'

"But the father said to his servants, 'Quick! Bring the best robe and put it on him. Put a ring on his finger and sandals on his feet. Bring the fattened calf and kill it. Let's have a feast and celebrate. For this son of mine was dead and is alive again; he was lost and is found.' So they began to celebrate." (Luke 15:11–24)

The unfaithful son's demand for his inheritance is unusual in the light of Jewish law (see Deut. 21:17). At that time there were two ways in which property could pass from father to son: by a will or by a gift during the father's lifetime. In the latter case, the father still received interest revenue from his estate. This meant the son could not dispose of the estate as he wished; he still had a responsibility to his father.

In the parable, the father went beyond his minimum legal obligations, allowing the son to use the estate as he pleased. The father knew it could mean losing his son, because famine was frequent in Palestine and living conditions were better in other parts of the world. This tells us that *our heavenly father never forces us into a relationship with him.* Floyd McClung writes, ". . . he [the father] wanted a relationship with his son more than forced obedience, but he must wait until he [the son] was ready for that."[2]

The son ran from his father into the arms of wild living. Men and women who do not know their father's love frequently fall into immorality. In part they hope to find the fatherly tenderness, love, and affection that they missed (or avoided) at home. But immorality never satisfies and always leads to ruin, which was the case for the son. He lost everything and was reduced to tending swine (which is humiliation to a Jew) and, finally, living with swine—a mark of abject poverty. When he came to his senses—actually, in the Hebrew and Aramaic that lay behind Luke's Greek rendering, this is an expression of repentance—the son decided to return home and throw himself at his father's mercy, begging for a job. Imagine the son's surprise upon returning home when his father ran to greet him, throwing his arms around him and kissing him, which was a sign of forgiveness (2 Sam. 14:33). From this we learn that *our heavenly Father is eager to have a relationship with us*. He wants to forgive our sin when we repent and return to him, and he wants us to experience his tenderness, love, and affection.

After cutting short his son's well-rehearsed repentance speech, the father threw a party, treating him as his son and not as a hired hand. In other words, *when we turn to him, our heavenly Father does not hold failure and sin against us*. In fact, the father gave his returned son a royal welcome! First came the best robe, a mark of distinction and the symbol of the advent of a new era. Next came a ring and sandals. In the ancient Near East a ring symbolized the bestowing of authority (see 1 Macc. 6:15). Sandals were a luxury, worn by free men. Here they meant the father did not consider his son a slave. Finally, the feast indicates our heavenly Father delights in the return of a wayward son or daughter and that he considers the return a special occasion.

Older Brother

But there is more to the parable. Jesus said:

> "Meanwhile, the older son was in the field. When he came near the house, he heard music and dancing. So he called one of the servants and asked him what was going on. 'Your brother has come,' he replied, 'and your father has killed the fattened calf because he has him back safe and sound.'
>
> "The older brother became angry and refused to go in. So his father went out and pleaded with him. But he answered his father, 'Look! All these years I've been slaving for you and never disobeyed

your orders. Yet you never gave me even a young goat so I could celebrate with my friends. But when this son of yours who has squandered your property with prostitutes comes home, you kill the fattened calf for him!'

"'My son,' the father said, 'you are always with me, and everything I have is yours. But we had to celebrate and be glad, because this brother of yours was dead and is alive again; he was lost and is found.'" (Luke 15:25–32)

The older brother's resentment was like the attitude of the Pharisees and teachers who opposed Jesus (Luke 15:2). Whereas the younger brother went looking for love in loose living, the older brother stayed at home and worked for his father's approval. But the harder he strove for love, the more angry he became. When the younger brother returned home to a celebration and fatherly acceptance, it was too much for the older brother to endure. His bitterness boiled over, revealing the depth of his alienation from his father. The father's response to the older brother was to affirm him ("My son . . .") and remind him that "everything I have is yours" (Luke 15:31).

I know many Christians who are like the older brother. They continually strive for their heavenly Father's love, yet they never attain the intimacy with God that would provide peace and affirmation. Over time they become bitter or burn out, drifting away from God or becoming angry legalists. There is no joy in their hearts, because every ounce of their strength is devoted to trying to earn the Father's love. They will continue to be drained until they experience again the spirit of adoption as God's sons and daughters. Yet our heavenly Father is saying, "My sons and daughters, all that I have is yours. Peace. Joy. Love. It's all yours. Just take it!"

This parable describes our heavenly Father in remarkable simplicity. He is full of goodness, graciousness, mercy, and abounding love. He rejoices over the return of the lost, and he makes available to us heavenly blessings as we turn to him in faith. That is the true picture of our heavenly Father and the kind of relationship with him he is inviting us to enjoy.

15

Touching the Father's Heart

Jesus revealed that fatherhood is the very essence of the Godhead. In fact, one of his primary purposes for coming was to show us a full revelation of his heavenly Father. "No one has ever seen God," the apostle John writes, "but God the One and Only [Jesus], who is at the Father's side, has made him known" (John 1:18).

Jesus attaches two significant qualifications to his understanding of divine fatherhood. First, when he speaks of God as the Father of others he almost always refers to his disciples. He taught that sin brought about a change in men and women, necessitating rebirth and reconciliation to God (John 3:3; 8:42; 14:6). In accordance with this, the apostles taught that it is only through Christ that we become children of God and are free to call God our Father (Gal. 4:6). We are *adopted* sons and daughters by grace: "For you did not receive a spirit that makes you a slave again to fear, but you received the Spirit of sonship [or *adoption*]. And by him we cry, '*Abba, Father*'" (Rom. 8:15; see also Gal. 3:25–26; Eph. 1:5).

Adoption, which was common among the Greeks and Romans, granted all the privileges of a natural son, including full inheritance rights. But heavenly adoption is superior to human adoption. It goes far beyond the legal rights of Greek and Roman adoption, promising that as we grow up in Christ we are *transformed* into our Father's likeness, taking on his attributes of love, mercy, compassion, and holiness (Rom. 8:29). Spiritual adoption also opens up an intimate, personal relationship with the Father in which we experience his love and affirmation and confidently pray to him in Jesus' name (John 14:14).

Intimacy

The second qualification provides the key for understanding the true nature of fatherhood: Jesus has a unique relationship with the Father, for unlike us, he is fully God. Jesus never suggests that the disciples' relationship with the Father is the same *kind* as his. He claims to be the preexistent eternal Son, equal in nature with the Father (John 1:14; 5:17–26; 8:54). The Father sent him for our salvation (John 3:36).

To touch the heart of fatherhood we need look no further than the Father's relationship with his Son (John 14:9–10). All earthly forms of fatherhood are but faint reflections in comparison to the original fatherhood between the First Person of the Trinity and his Son. Their relationship is the ideal, the pattern, the *basis* for our experience of the Father. In response to Jesus' teaching that "No one comes to the Father except through me," Philip said, "Lord, show us the Father and that will be enough for us." Jesus answered:

> "Don't you know me, Philip, even after I have been among you
> such a long time? Anyone who has seen me has seen the Father.
> How can you say, 'Show us the Father'? Don't you believe that I
> am in the Father, and that the Father is in me? The words I say to
> you are not just my own. Rather, it is the Father, living in me, who
> is doing his work." (John 14:6–10)

Jesus stresses the intimate connection between the Father and himself. "Look at me," he says, "and you know the Father. I bring you a full revelation of the Father."

His prayer life was one of constant communion with his Father (Matt. 14:23; Mark 1:35; Luke 5:16), a privilege that Jesus taught his disciples was available to them also. "But when you pray," he said, "go into your room, close the door and pray to your Father, who is unseen. Then your Father, who sees what is done in secret, will reward you." Then he offered the Lord's Prayer as the pattern for effective prayer: "This, then, is how you should pray: 'Our Father in heaven, hallowed be your name . . .'" (Matt. 6:6, 9). Jesus does not tell the disciples to call God a "Higher Power," "The Ground of Being," or "Holy Exalted One." Instead, he instructs them to address God as Father.

Teaching us to pray to our "heavenly Father" reveals several aspects of God's nature that should astound us. First, he wants fellowship with us and he is available for intimate communion. He is the perfect Dad, always there for his kids. In fact he is so close, so available, that it is fair to say that *he* is pursuing us, continually drawing us to him. Scripture emphasizes our duty to pray, for we have been created in Christ to know and be known by the Father (Luke 18:1; Eph. 6:18; Phil. 4:6; 1 Thess. 5:17).

Praying to our heavenly Father also reassures us that we need not fear rejection when we turn to God. He is always there, and when we repent from sin he will forgive and receive us (Ps. 130:3–4). Like any loving father, he may have to discipline us, but even discipline is motivated by love and by the goal of our maturity: "Our fathers disciplined us for a little while as they thought best; but God disciplines us for our good, that we may share in his holiness" (Heb. 12:10).

Remembering that God is also Jesus' Father and loves Jesus deeply helps us to know what to pray about. Jesus wants us to pray that the love that the Father has for him would be felt in our hearts, that love for Jesus should be our ultimate motivation (John 17:26). Here is a prayer I suggest you pray daily: "Father, put in my heart the same love for Jesus that you have for him. O Father, that's what I desire."

Finally, praying to our heavenly Father means there is no request or topic too trivial to talk with God about. He likes it that way.

Think about it; he cares about the big things in life—marriage, job, relationships—and he cares about the little things too—a flat tire, exams, buying a new dress. Loving fathers know that "little" things are not so little to their children; our heavenly Father listens intently to *anything* we approach him with, knowing it is important to us or we would not bring it to him.

Obedience

Jesus' relationship with his Father also reveals God's expectation of his kids. It all comes down to one word: *obedience*.

A brief survey of John's Gospel illustrates how Jesus related to the Father. Jesus often mentions that he depended on the Father and that he came "to do the will of him who sent me and to finish his work" (John 4:34; see also 6:38). "I seek not to please myself," Jesus said, "but him who sent me" (John 5:30). He listened to his Father and told the world what he heard (John 8:26; 12:49–50). He worked diligently at fulfilling the work God had for him (John 9:4) and thus brought glory to the Father. He claimed to do what his Father did—including miracles (John 10:37–38). He loved the Father and did exactly what he commanded him to do (John 14:31). Jesus tied love and obedience together in John 15:9–10: "As the Father has loved me, so have I loved you. Now remain in my love. If you obey my commands, you will remain in my love, just as I have obeyed my Father's commands and remain in his love."

Jesus says the key to remaining in his love is obedience, and he has modeled obedience for us in how he related to his Father. Further, in John 14:21, Jesus said, "He who loves me will be loved by my Father." The apostle John reiterates this in 1 John 5:3, "This is love for God: to obey his commands." Lest his readers think this is an impossible task, John adds an important qualifier: "And his commands are not burdensome, for everyone born of God overcomes the world." The message seems clear enough: to know the love of our heavenly Father we must be obedient sons and daughters.

How important is obedience to the Christian life? Peter says we have been chosen "according to the foreknowledge of God the Father, through the sanctifying work of the Spirit, *for obedience to Jesus Christ* and sprinkling by his blood" (1 Pet. 1:2). All three Persons of the Trinity are mentioned in this remarkable verse. Father, Son, and Holy Spirit have orchestrated our redemption so that we may be obedient to Christ.

We enter the kingdom of God now as we submit to him, and we submit by doing the will of the Father (Matt. 7:21), obeying his commandments (Matt. 5:19), and having the humble attitude of little children (Matt. 18:3). Our success in life and our walk to maturity are by-products of cooperating with the Father's will on earth. We cooperate with God's will by submitting to Jesus, which is the topic of Part V.

PART V

Submitting to Christ

16

Who Do You Say I Am?

The two most important questions in life are "Who is God?" and "What does he want me to do?" Our answers to these questions are only as reliable as our sources. We have seen that Scripture is the only ultimately reliable witness. So our answers must come from Scripture.

A few years after I became a Christian, I bumped into an old friend from the music business. Someone had told him that I had had a weird religious experience, and he was interested in learning more about it.

"I became a Christian," I said. Then I began telling him who Jesus is and how we can know him.

"Excuse me," he interrupted, "but I've just read a book called *The Passover Plot*. The author believes Jesus did not die on the cross. He says Jesus planned his own arrest and faked his crucifixion and his resurrection. He arranged to be drugged before he went on the cross. He never actually died, which explains his so-called post-resurrection appearances. According to the book, Jesus was not God, he was a fraud."[1]

My friend knew that if Jesus is not who he claimed to be, then Christianity loses its power. If, on the other hand, Jesus is acknowledged as the resurrected Son of God, there is no excuse for not submitting to him. This is not merely an intellectual exercise. Our eternal fate is determined by our response to the historical Jesus.

After he finished his argument I pointed toward the nearby beach. "Do you see the beach?" I asked.

"Yes."

"Can you see the Pacific Ocean?" I knew he could not, because from where we were standing the water was just out of view.

"No," he replied.

"Okay, let's say you were visiting here for the first time. Could you believe the Pacific is just over the horizon, even though you never actually saw it?"

"Yes. Of course I could."

"Do you know why you could believe it's there?" I asked, not giving him an opportunity to answer. "You'd know it's there because you hear it and because you see people coming from it who are wearing wet bathing suits and carrying surfboards. And if you were to ask them how they got wet, they would tell you an ocean is there.

"It's the same with Jesus. You can hear about him from the Bible, you can see people whose lives have been changed through knowing him—that's what changed me—and you can hear reliable witnesses tell you that he's for real. The Bible would pass the test as a reliable witness in a court of law, and I can tell you from my experience that Jesus is alive today. We're standing here and you're telling me that Jesus is not God—but I'm all wet! I just came from him."

My friend was not convinced by this argument at that time, but he admitted that I gave him much to think about. Later he became a Christian and told me afterward that he could not forget my illustration.

Since the 1960s the *The Passover Plot,* like so many similar books, has been sentenced to collect dust on the shelves of secondhand bookstores. But confusion about the person and work of Jesus remains, even among Christians.

The Central Question

Even during Jesus' life there was debate about who he was. Jesus once asked the disciples, "Who do people say I am?" (Mark 8:27–30).

The people held a variety of opinions. They were actually rather flattering. "John the Baptist," said some. "Elijah," suggested others. "One of the prophets," said yet others. Jesus' contemporaries were placing him in the company of their greatest heroes, Israel's "hall of fame." Like many people today, most thought Jesus was a prominent man, perhaps one of the greatest men who ever lived. But their answers were wrong, just as many people's answers today are wrong.

Recently many Christians marched outside cinemas across North America to protest against the showing of the film *The Last Temptation of Christ*. The film, based on Nikos Kazantzakis' 1955 best-selling novel, is one response to Christ's question, "Who do you say I am?" Christ is presented as a weak Roman collaborator who is unsure about his message and mission.

Richard N. Ostling, writing in *Time* magazine, said that Jesus' question "is today not only at the heart of Hollywood's latest controversy but also at the center of equally bitter, though less publicized, disputes among scholars concerning the life of Jesus."[2]

Ostling outlines a few of the contemporary interpretations of Jesus, all of which have made their way to some degree into popular thinking. For example, there is the itinerant sage Jesus, a wandering moralist not unlike Gandhi. Or there is the inspired rabbi Jesus, "a rabbinical genius whose teachings were very much in keeping with the liberal Jewish scholarship of his day." Every few years scholars who reject large portions of the Gospels propose a new "Jesus." One group of professors, known as the Jesus Seminar, meets twice a year to vote on the authenticity of Christ's sayings in the New

Testament. They have decided, for example, that Christ did say, "Blessed are the poor" but did not say, "Blessed are the meek."

Jesus was grieved that the crowds had so little insight into his true identity. In his disappointment it was natural that he would turn to his disciples. "But what about you?" Jesus asked them. "Who do *you* say I am?" (Matt. 16:15).

Simon Peter responded: "You are the Christ, the Son of the living God" (Matt. 16:16). "Christ" was an official name, meaning "the Anointed One." The Anointed One was to bring God's reign to earth and possess the Holy Spirit (1 Sam. 24:10; 2 Sam. 7; Isa. 61:1; Zech. 4:1–6). "The Son of the living God" was a title of the Messiah, a heavenly King come to set up his kingdom on earth (2 Sam. 7:14; Ps. 89:27). In short, Peter was claiming that Jesus was God himself.

"Blessed are you," Jesus said, "for this was not revealed to you by man, but by my Father in heaven" (Matt. 16:17). Jesus' remark tells us two things. First, we are blessed by God when we know who Jesus truly is. Second, we can know who Jesus is only through God's revelation. Let us take a look at what God has revealed to us about Jesus in the next chapter.

17

Fully God

What does God's word say about who Jesus is?

First and foremost, it says that Jesus is fully God. This is clearly stated in many passages. John says, "In the beginning was the Word"—later, in verse 14, John identifies "the Word" as Jesus—"and the Word was with God, and *the Word was God*" (John 1:1). Paul says Christ *"is God over all"* (Rom. 9:5) and tells us to look forward to "the glorious appearing of our *great God* and Savior, Jesus Christ" (Titus 2:13). He says that in Christ, *"all the fullness of the Deity lives in bodily form"* (Col. 2:9).[1]

On many occasions Jesus himself claimed to be God. In John 5:17 he tells the Jews, who were persecuting him for healing an invalid on the Sabbath, "My Father is always at his work to this very day, and I, too, am working." The Jews "tried all the harder to kill him" because "he was even calling God his own Father, making himself equal with God" (5:18). Some critics maintain that the Jews drew the wrong conclusion: that what Jesus meant by claiming God's fatherhood did not imply equality with God. But if this were so, why did Jesus not correct the Jews? Apparently he endorsed their conclusion.

In the account of the rigged trial before the Sanhedrin, the high priest asks Jesus, "Are you the Christ, the Son of the Blessed One?" (Mark 14:61). Not only does Jesus claim messiahship, but the way he answers makes it clear that he thinks the Messiah is God. Jesus says, "I am . . . And you will see the Son of Man sitting at the right hand of the Mighty One and coming on the clouds of heaven" (Mark 14:62). The words "I am" solemnly echo Exodus 3:14, in which God tells Moses his name: "This is what you are to say to the Israelites: 'I AM has sent me to you.'" "I AM" was the name by which God was known and worshiped in Israel, and Jesus claimed to be the "I AM." The high priest clearly understood that Jesus was claiming to be God; he tore his clothing and said, "You have [all] heard the blasphemy" (Mark 14:64).

Jesus not only claimed to be God, he acted like God. We are so familiar with the biblical miracles that frequently we fail to realize their significance as authenticating signs of Jesus' divinity.[2] Jesus demonstrated his power over nature, disease, death, and demons. The number and extent of his miracles are staggering. He walked on water and calmed the seas (Matt. 8:23–27; Mark 6:45–52). He turned water into wine (John 2:1–11) and fed five thousand people from five loaves and two fish (Mark 6:30–44). He also forgave sin (Mark 2:5)—and who but God can forgive sin (Mark 2:7)?

When Thomas fell at his feet and said, "My Lord and my God!" (John 20:28), Jesus blessed him for recognizing he was God and worshiping him (John 20:29). The name "Lord," which comes from *Adonai* in the Hebrew Old Testament, refers to authoritative ownership and is approximately equal to "God." Jesus was well aware of the seriousness of being worshiped (Matt. 4:10). When he received Thomas's worship he implicitly claimed deity.

Knowing God or Knowing Notions?

Knowing that Jesus is God is not the same thing as knowing God. Years ago I had an experience that brought this truth home to me. One morning I received a call from a new convert explaining that there were many warrants out for his arrest in Bakersfield, California, a city approximately a hunderd miles from Yorba Linda. He asked me if I would accompany him as he drove there to turn himself in to the police and clear up his record. I agreed to go with him.

Very early the next morning, while it was still dark, we drove over a stretch of highway called "the grapevine," a dangerous road that goes through a mountain pass. Just as we were entering the grapevine a violent rainstorm hit; we could hardly see fifty feet ahead. On one turn the headlights illumined a sign that said, "Jesus Saves." As we inched past the sign, a shadowy figure appeared on the road. It was a hitchhiker; I decided to pull over and pick him up.

We opened the passenger door to be greeted by a grotesque, malformed man. He said, "I need a lift."

"Jump in."

He fell on the back seat, and within a matter of seconds he was fast asleep. He had not had a bath in days, and his body odor was overpowering. I wondered if I had not made a mistake in offering him a ride.

We pulled into Bakersfield around dawn and found a restaurant. The hitchhiker disappeared into the men's room to clean up, and when he returned to the table we offered to pay for his breakfast. He accepted. Then we asked him if we could pray for him.

He asked, "Are you Christians?"

"Yes," we said. "Are you?"

"Yes," he said. "I just became one this morning, in the back seat of your car."

We asked him to tell us his story.

"Two days ago I was living in Los Angeles and I heard a man say, 'Jesus saves.' I could tell he believed what he said, so I decided to go home to northern California and talk to my brother. I thought he could help me make sense of it. When I got on the highway and it rained so hard and I saw the sign that says, 'Jesus Saves,' I thought, 'If Jesus is real and can save me from my sins, he can save me from this rain. God, if you really love me, have someone stop and pick me up.' Then you came, and I gave my heart to Jesus as I fell asleep."

He was a very simple man, quite limited both intellectually and emotionally. But he learned something about God that night, and he used his knowledge of God as a launching point to knowing God himself. As we continued to talk that morning I could see that his new faith was indeed genuine. His belief in Christ's deity went beyond intellectual assent; he trusted Jesus with his heart and was a transformed man.

The Significance of Jesus' Deity

What does it mean to us that Jesus is God? First, it makes Jesus an appropriate object of true worship. Paul says, "We know that an idol is nothing at all in the world and that there is no God but one" (1 Cor. 8:4). An idol is *anything* that replaces God. If we were to deny Christ's deity, yet worship him, we would be guilty of idolatry. A "Jesus" who was not divine would be an idol. But the Jesus presented to us in the Bible is the very incarnation of God himself.

Second, Christ's sacrifice on the cross was of infinite value because, as God, Christ had eternal attributes. We were utterly incapable of paying the price we owed God for our sin. The psalmist is blunt: "No man can redeem the life of another or give to God a ransom for him—the ransom for a life is costly, no payment is ever enough—that he should live on forever and not see decay" (Ps. 49:7–9). However, the Son of God could pay the price, and he did. It came at a high cost, but now we can be free from the sin and guilt that tear men and women apart.

Don Richardson's story *Peace Child* communicates many of the elements of redemption. Back in 1962 Don and his wife, Carol, went as missionaries to the Sawi people of the former Netherlands, New Guinea (now called Irian Jaya, Indonesia). The Sawi, still living in the Stone Age and isolated from all except nearby tribes, were headhunting cannibals. Individual Sawi tribes were locked in a centuries-long treadmill of war in which they tried to outdo each other in treachery, murder, and revenge.

Temporary peace came only when a son from one tribe, referred to as a "peace child," was given to another as a peace offering. The tribes' two leaders would exchange sons and their own names. As you can imagine, the parents who gave up sons suffered greatly, and the ceremony was accompanied by much grief. After the exchange the people from each tribe would gather around and lay hands on their respective peace child, thus sealing their acceptance of the peace. Then the two tribes would come together and exchange names and gifts, symbolizing peace and unity.

However, the peace was usually short-lived, for the death of a peace child—not an uncommon occurrence in the disease-infested jungles of New Guinea—released a tribe from its peace commitment. Revenge, treachery, and cannibalism quickly set in again. Of course, Don Richardson saw in the peace child a powerful analogy to Jesus, the perfect and eternal Peace Child. He told the Sawi:

> "I kept saying to myself, 'O that they could make peace without this painful giving of a son!' But you [the Sawis] kept saying, 'There is no other way!' . . . You were right!
>
> "When I stopped to think about it, I realized you and your ancestors are not the only ones who found that peace required a peace child. *Myao Kodon,* the Spirit whose message I bear, has declared the same thing—true peace can never come without a peace child! Never!
>
> "Because *Myao Kodon* wants men to find peace with Him and with each other, He decided to choose a once-for-all [peace] child good enough and strong enough to establish peace, not just for a while, but forever! The problem was, whom should He choose? For among all human children, there was no son good enough or strong enough to be an eternal [peace]."

Richardson went on to describe how Jesus was God's Peace Child who died and was raised from the dead in order to give us eternal life and peace. Through his teaching on the Peace Child, many of the Sawi eventually became Christians.[3]

Third, because Jesus is God, we know God himself truly feels our pain. In Christ, God himself experienced what it was to be friendless, hungry, naked, beaten, and murdered. This is a God who understands *everything* about us; he feels our pain, for he has experienced it. John Stott writes, "The real sting of suffering is not misfortune itself, nor even the pain of it or the injustice of it, but the apparent God-forsakenness of it. Pain is endurable, but the seeming indifference of God is not."[4] But God truly does feel our pain, and that should comfort us when we suffer.

Finally, Christ is able to apply the fruits of his accomplished works to those who trust in him, because as God he has the power to freely give his grace. Jesus is able to lavish his grace and forgiveness on us (Eph. 1:7–8; 2:4–10), because as God he is seated "at [the Father's] right hand in the heavenly realms, far above all rule and authority, power and dominion . . ." (Eph. 1:20–21). As God he possesses the power to conquer Satan (Heb. 2:14), perform miracles that display his Father's glory (John 11:4, 40), conquer death (John 10:18), and save us (Acts 2:24). I will have much more to say about Christ's victory over sin, Satan, and death in Part VI.

18

Fully Human

Some people think of Jesus as God in a human body, devoid of human emotions, intellect, will, and soul. But Scripture teaches that he was *fully* human. His conception was supernatural (Luke 1:35), but his birth was natural (Luke 2:6–7)—though, of course, the circumstances surrounding it were exceptional (Luke 2:8–20). He grew up in a fashion common to all men and women (Luke 2:52) and expressed natural human emotions (John 11:33, 35; 13:23). For example, he experienced love and compassion (Matt. 9:36) and righteous anger (Matt. 21:13; Mark 3:5). He wept when he learned of a close friend's death (John 11:35), and his "heart was troubled" shortly before his arrest (John 12:27). He also had physical needs, like thirst (John 19:28) and hunger (Matt. 4:2). He became weary and needed sleep (John 4:6; Matt. 8:24). In sum, Jesus was a complete man—body, soul, and spirit (1 John 1:1–4).

The writers of the New Testament were as intent on preserving Christ's full humanity as they were his deity. Peter made much of the fact that Jesus was a descendant of Abraham (Acts 3:25), and Luke refers to David as Jesus' "father" (Luke 1:32). Paul said Jesus was "born of a woman" (Gal. 4:4).

As a man, Jesus was tempted in every way that we are: "Because he himself suffered when he was tempted, he is able to help those who are being tempted" (Heb. 2:18; see also 4:15). When we are distressed and turn to Jesus, he understands everything we are struggling with. He was "the Word made flesh" who "made his dwelling among us" (John 1:14). Moreover, as a man Christ bore the wrath of God for our sins and freed us from Satan's tyranny. "Since the children have flesh and blood," the writer to the Hebrews says, "he too shared in their humanity so that by his death he might destroy him who holds the power of death—that is, the devil—and free those who all their lives were held in slavery by their fear of death" (Heb. 2:14–15). Later in the same chapter of Hebrews it says, "For this reason he had to be made like his brothers in every way . . . [so that] he might make atonement for the sins of the people" (v. 17; see also 9:22).

However, there is one significant difference between Christ's humanity and ours: though he was tempted in every way, he was without sin (Heb. 4:15; 1 John 3:5). He never gave in to Satan. At one point in his life Jesus asked, "Can any of you prove me guilty of sin?" (John 8:46). Of course, the answer was no. Satan had "no hold" on Jesus (John 14:30). Because he never sinned, Jesus is the ideal man, our pattern for living (2 Cor. 3:18). Paul encouraged the Corinthians to follow his example "as I follow the example of Christ" (1 Cor. 11:1).

One Person

As God and man Jesus is able to act as a mediator between his Father and us (1 Tim. 2:5; Heb. 2:11–18), so we can enjoy the full benefits of his forgiveness and grace, and a personal relationship with the Father. A good analogy for how Jesus mediates between God and humanity is a bridge. Because Jesus is divine, the bridge is perfectly connected to God; and because he is fully man, the bridge is equally connected to us. It is a bridge that cannot be broken, and it is always open for men and women to cross over into a full relationship with their heavenly Father.

Though Jesus is God and man, he is not two people. He has one personality. The theologians say he has two natures in perfect union. The Chalcedonian Definition of 451 made it clear that Jesus was "at once complete in Godhead and complete in manhood, truly God and truly man, . . . coming together to form one person and subsistence, not as parted or separated into two persons, but one and the same Son and Only-begotten God the Word, Lord Jesus Christ." That is quite a mouthful, but it is one of the best summary statements of who Jesus is—two natures, one Person. One author describes this union as two "Whats" and one "Who"—fully God, fully man, one Person.[1]

Such a unique being required a miraculous birth. From his conception Jesus was God; he had already existed from eternity as the Word of God and as the Son of God. He was conceived by God through the work of the Holy Spirit in his mother, Mary (Luke 1:35). Through the Holy Spirit, who always plays a role in beginning life, he became a man, while remaining God.

This is why Jesus was born of Mary. Though it was a miraculous conception, he was a man from the very start, and Mary was his mother (Luke 1:43). It was a normal birth; Mary felt real labor pains, and Jesus undoubtedly cried like any newborn baby. Mary was a virgin at the time of his conception because God was Jesus' Father.

It took great humility for God to become a man. That is the topic of the next chapter.

19

Putting On Humility

There is a passage of Scripture that sheds light on *how* the two natures come together in one Person. Paul says, "[Jesus], being in very nature God, did not consider equality with God something to be grasped, but made himself nothing, taking the very nature of a servant, being made in human likeness" (Phil. 2:6–7). "Look, Philippians," Paul could be paraphrased, "Jesus didn't demand his own rights but looked out for others instead" (see also 2 Cor. 8:9). This was all the more remarkable, Paul says, because Jesus was in his "very nature" God. Yet he laid his divine attributes aside and, instead, voluntarily lived under human conditions so that he could fulfill his unselfish purpose to save humanity.

Jesus took on "the very nature of a servant" (v. 7). The expression "the very nature" means that Jesus did not just take on the outward appearance of a servant; he took on the full attributes of humanity in becoming an *actual* servant. B. B. Warfield writes, "The Lord of the world became a servant in the world; he whose right it was to rule took obedience as his life-characteristic."[1]

The phrase "made himself nothing" in Philippians 2:7 can also be translated "emptied himself." The Greek word from which "emptied" is translated is *kenosis*. Its precise meaning is unclear. Some theologians interpret *kenosis* as meaning Christ completely emptied himself of deity while on earth, so he was limited to the knowledge and abilities of an ordinary man. This comes dangerously close to denying Christ's deity.

Others interpret *kenosis* as meaning Jesus retained his divine nature but emptied himself of his divine *prerogatives*—the high position and glory of deity. This interpretation is probably closer to the truth. Jesus did not give up his deity, but he *did* lay aside his glory (John 17:5) and submit to the humiliation of becoming a man (2 Cor. 8:9). The idea behind *kenosis* is not that Jesus took on humanity and took off deity as though they were coats that could be changed; it is that he took on humanity while remaining fully God.

The *kenosis*—or emptying—of Christ is not merely a piece of theological speculation; it is a power point. For the fundamental issue of this passage is that we are called to imitate Christ's humility, summed up earlier in Philippians 2:3-4: "Do nothing out of selfish ambition or vain conceit, but in humility consider others better than yourselves. Each of you should look not only to your own interests, but also to the interests of others." Jesus taught that humility is a hallmark of vital Christianity (see Mark 10:41-45; John 13:12-17), and he exemplified it by emptying himself of deity and becoming a man. If Christ, who is in the form of God, chooses not to look to his own interests, how can we help but choose to turn from our sinful nature, a nature that is marked by "selfish ambition" and "vain conceit"?

Jesus emptied himself and took on the nature of a servant in order "to give his life as a ransom for many" (Matt. 20:28). We are called to do the same (John 20:21). Jesus' servanthood clarifies the true nature of every Christian's calling: to pour out our lives for the salvation of the world.

Note how contrary the idea of servanthood is to the world's values. In the world, we are encouraged to be true to our feelings, to make self-development our highest goal in life, and to throw off restrictions or authority that inhibit personal fulfillment. But the Lord says, "Whoever finds his life will lose it, and whoever loses his life for my sake will find it" (Matt. 10:39). The apostles took Jesus' *kenosis* to heart: with the lone exception of John, every one of them was martyred on account of the gospel.

Childlike Faith

Christ's *kenosis* touches on one of the most precious of biblical truths. But we can only experience this truth if we have a childlike faith in God. F. Kefa Sempangi, a Ugandan pastor who barely escaped death under Idi Amin's persecution in the early 1970s, beautifully captures this sense in his wonderful book *A Distant Grief.* He writes about a hurtful change that came over him shortly after coming to the United States and enrolling in an evangelical seminary:

> In Uganda, Penina [Kefa's wife] and I read the Bible for hope and life. We read to hear God's promises, to hear His commands and obey them. There had been no time for argument and no time for religious discrepancies or doubts.
>
> Now, in the security of a new life and with the reality of death fading from mind, I found myself reading Scripture to analyze texts and speculate about meaning. I came to enjoy abstract theological discussions with my fellow students and, while these discussions were intellectually refreshing, it wasn't long before our fellowship revolved around ideas rather than the work of God in our lives. It was not the blood of Jesus Christ that gave us unity, but our agreement on doctrinal issues. We came together not for confession and forgiveness but for debate.

This change in attitude toward God had its greatest impact in Kefa's prayer life: "God Himself had become a distant figure. He had become a subject of debate, an abstract category. I no longer prayed to Him as a living Father but as an impersonal being who did not mind my inattention and unbelief."[2]

When he realized how far he had drifted from God due to theological speculations, Kefa repented of his attitudes. Immediately his prayer life was renewed. Thereafter he began consciously to submit himself moment by moment to the living God, meekly accepting what God said in his word. He learned a valuable lesson: returning to our first love usually means simplifying the way we think about God, accepting his mysteries and receiving their benefits.

We have spoken about the deity and humanity of Jesus Christ. These are difficult concepts to fathom. I encourage you to accept the understanding that Jesus has given you about his natures and Person and then cultivate a relationship with him that is based more on his promises and commands than on your questions. Go ahead and ask questions—but be careful not to allow them to cloud your relationship with God.

The Father's Purpose

I began Part V by asking two questions: Who is God? and What does he want me to do? The answer to the latter question is found in understanding the purpose for which his Father sent Jesus to earth. Consider these verses:

> And he [God] made known to us the mystery of his will according to his good pleasure, which he purposed in Christ, to be put into effect when the times will have reached their fulfillment—to bring all things in heaven and on earth together under one head, even Christ. (Eph. 1:9–10)

> Then the end will come, when he [Jesus] hands over the kingdom to God the Father after he has destroyed all dominion, authority and power. For he must reign until he has put all his enemies under his feet. The last enemy to be destroyed is death. For he "has put everything under his feet." Now when it says that "everything" has been put under him, it is clear that this does not include God himself, who put everything under Christ. (1 Cor. 15:24–27)

> Therefore God [the Father] exalted him [Jesus] to the highest place and gave him the name that is above every name, that at the name of Jesus every knee should bow, in heaven and on earth and under

the earth, and every tongue confess that Jesus Christ is Lord, to the glory of God the Father. (Phil. 2:9–11)

The Father has a plan for Jesus: That every created being will "confess that Jesus Christ is Lord." The Father wants to bring glory to the Son by establishing him as the preeminent Ruler of the universe, the absolute Lord of all. How he accomplishes his plan is the topic of Part VI.

PART VI

Taking Up the Cross

20

The Father's Sacrificial Love

One of the most heartbreaking stories that Kefa Sempangi tells of Uganda under Idi Amin's reign of terror involves Joseph "Jolly Joe" Kiwanuka. Before Amin came to power in January 1971, Kiwanuka was one of Uganda's wealthiest and most influential citizens, an outspoken atheist and humanist.

Amin's brutality against his fellow countrymen shattered Kiwanuka's faith in humanity. Broken and desperate, Kiwanuka visited Kefa's Redeemed Church and later converted to Christ. Shortly after his conversion he told the congregation, "From the beginning I have been looking for a kingdom . . . for a kingdom of freedom."[1] Kiwanuka was a thoroughly changed man.

Until the autumn of 1973 Kiwanuka spoke out boldly for Christ and used his few remaining political connections to save many lives. Living in a nation shrouded with death, Kiwanuka knew where to find life: "It is because of the Resurrection that we are free. We are not slaves to this life or to our fear of death. We are slaves to Jesus Christ and He has risen from the grave."[2]

In December 1973 Kiwanuka was forced to flee Uganda to neighboring Kenya. But within a few days Amin's agents kidnapped him, bringing him by force to the Makindye Prison in Uganda. After being tortured for several days Kiwanuka was brought before

Amin, who began beating him with a small hammer. As Kiwanuka fell to the ground he prayed aloud for Amin, which caused the dictator to fly into a rage, grab a sledgehammer, and kill him with one crushing blow. Amin then severed Kiwanuka's head and practiced blood rituals over his body.

Kefa Sempangi had himself earlier narrowly escaped Amin's terror and fled to Amsterdam. Kiwanuka's death hurt Kefa deeply; he plunged into severe depression. But then God gave him a vision in which he saw Jesus at the grave of Lazarus, weeping with Mary. The body of Lazarus, who had been dead for four days, was in a state of stinking decay. Jesus looked death in the eye, knowing that some day he too would enter a grave. But Jesus would rise from the grave and triumph over death. At that moment Kefa knew that Kiwanuka was raised with Jesus, that death had no hold over Jolly Joe.

Kefa realized that in his grief he had fallen into the trap of seeing himself as more compassionate than God. He had forgotten the cross: "[God's] own Son had suffered the defeat of physical pain and death, and still suffered with the suffering of his children. . . . What Kiwanuka and thousands of other martyrs had sown in tears, they, and the church with them, would reap in joy."[3]

Joseph Kiwanuka's blood is a testimony to the power of God's righteousness and mercy. Kiwanuka was willing to forfeit his life and exhibit great courage—even to forgive and to pray for Amin!—because he knew reconciliation with God.

Yet, as heroic as Kiwanuka's death was, it could never be the basis for Amin's (or anyone else's) receiving forgiveness and reconciliation with God. Achieving that reconciliation was God's purpose in sending Jesus to die on the cross.

Jesus' death on the cross is central to everything he accomplished. "The cross" encompasses the death, burial, resurrection, and ascension of Jesus—the very heart of his work on earth.

In the minds of the first Christians the cross was a symbol of all that is holy and precious. This is remarkable, because previously the cross had been considered the most vile and repulsive of objects. Rome considered crucifixion too base for it's own citizens' punishment. According to tradition Peter, a noncitizen, was crucified; Paul, a Roman citizen, was beheaded.

Love

How could a loving Father plan his own Son's humiliation? First and foremost, God was motivated by love for you and me, because he *is* love (1 John 4:8, 16). "For God so loved the world," the apostle John writes, "that he gave his one and only Son . . ." (John 3:16; see also Rom. 5:8).

Why did he allow Jesus to undergo the indignity of the cross? One of the greatest stories of the Old Testament describes God's testing of Abraham. God said, "Take your son, your only son, Isaac, whom you love, and go to the region of Moriah. Sacrifice him there as a burnt offering . . ." (Gen. 22:2). Think of the impact that God's words had on Abraham. He was an old man, and Isaac was his child of promise, the apple of his eye. He loved him more than anything in the world. But God said, "Kill the boy. Now. Obey."

We often forget that Isaac was old enough to understand what was happening. He helped carry the wood up the mountain for his own sacrifice. He even asked Abraham where the sacrifice was. "God himself will provide the lamb" was Abraham's reply (Gen. 22:8). Then Isaac was bound and placed on the wood, under the shadow of Abraham's raised knife. Only at the last instant did God intervene. "Do not lay a hand on the boy," an angel told Abraham (Gen. 22:12).

Abraham and Isaac are foreshadowings of the Father and the Son, of what God fulfilled at the cross centuries later. But God did not require of Abraham and Isaac what he required of himself. Isaac was spared; Jesus was crucified. How great is the love of the Father for us!

Necessity

But it was not only the Father's love that sent Jesus to the cross, it was also his justice. To understand God's justice, we must understand his wrath. It may be difficult to think of the God of love as being a God of wrath, but Scripture tells us this is so. Romans 1:18

says, "The wrath of God is being revealed from heaven against all the godlessness and wickedness of men who suppress the truth by their wickedness" (see also Eph. 2:3).

God's wrath is not a petulant, spiteful, irrational burst of anger such as Idi Amin exhibited when he killed Joseph Kiwanuka. It is a holy, just revulsion against what is contrary to and opposes God's nature and will. John Stott defines God's wrath as his "personal, righteous, constant hostility to evil, his settled refusal to compromise with it, and his resolve instead to condemn it." Yet at the same time Stott notes that God's wrath "is not incompatible with his love."[4]

We know that when we sin we break God's law. But sin is not only a crime against God's law; it is also an offense against God's love. Sin breaks God's heart (Gen. 6:6). What is more, there is nothing *we* can do to remove the chasm between God and us. Even if we were able to live perfect lives after we became conscious of our sins, we could not take away the guilt of our earlier sin. We sin against God's heart, and only his free act of forgiveness can restore our relationship. The cross is that free act.

The cross makes it possible for God simultaneously to take our sin seriously and to extend his love to us. God's justice demands our death as punishment for our sin, yet his love desires our justification. The cross is his solution: ". . . he did it [sent Jesus to the cross] to demonstrate his justice at the present time, so as to be just and the one who justifies those who have faith in Jesus" (Rom. 3:26). Mercy and justice meet at the cross. God's love cannot operate apart from the cross, for forgiveness cannot come from anywhere except the cross.

The depth of meaning of the cross touches on the very nature of God, so we should not be surprised to find it difficult to fathom the truths surrounding it. The New Testament writers use words like atonement, redemption, reconciliation, justification, propitiation, and regeneration to explain the meaning of the cross. Understanding the significance of these words today requires some historical background. Each highlights a different aspect of the cross. Together they form a fine tapestry of salvation. In the next two chapters, we will take a look at some of these words and what they signify.

21

Under the Blood

Hebrews 2:17 says Jesus came "that he might make *atonement* for the sins of the people" (see also 1 John 2:2). The word "atonement" means "a making at one." It points to the process by which God brings us into union with himself. The atonement makes us one with God through turning aside God's wrath and making him favorably inclined toward us. I think of the atonement as the answer to two dilemmas:

Dilemma 1: Because men and women are sinful, we cannot have fellowship with a holy God.

Dilemma 2: Because God is holy, he can have nothing to do with sinful men and women.

The solution is forgiveness. God no longer holds our sins against us, making it possible for him to initiate a relationship with us without violating his holy nature. The key is that Christ uniquely takes our place (he is our substitute, John 11:50; 1 Tim. 2:6), enduring God's wrath for us. Jesus also represents us on the cross (2 Cor. 5:14), so that as we identify with him, the benefits of his death are applied to us.

To first-century Jewish Christians "atonement" brought to mind the sacrificial rites of the Old Testament. When Christ was said to atone for our sins, they thought of him as a blood sacrifice that removes sin. When John the Baptist calls Jesus "the Lamb of God, who takes away the sin of the world" (John 1:29), or when it is said that Jesus died "on behalf of" human beings, or when Hebrews 7:27 describes Jesus as a high priest sacrificing himself, this is the language of atonement. The concept is that instead of a sinner dying for his or her own sins, a substitute (normally an animal) is offered and dies in his or her place. The blood poured out represents the life that has been sacrificed and becomes a symbol of all the benefits of the sacrifice. Western Christians today, with no personal background of blood sacrifice, find the idea difficult to grasp. But to New Testament listeners it was clear.

The Greek word from which "atonement" comes may also be translated "propitiation," a word that adds a significant twist. Like atonement, propitiation means that at the cross the wrath of God is turned away from human beings, due to the substitutionary offering of Christ. But propitiation implies that God's wrath is removed by the offering of a *gift*. Looked at this way, the blood of Christ appeases God's wrath. Romans 3:25 in the Authorized Version says, "God hath set forth [Jesus] to be a *propitiation* through faith in his blood, to declare his righteousness for the remission of sins that are past, through the forbearance of God."

The bottom line of the atonement is this: The blood of Christ both covers our sin and guilt (atonement) *and* satisfies God's righteous anger (propitiation). Both are required for us to have union with God.

Redemption

Originally "redemption" referred to the paying of a price (called a ransom) to gain the release for prisoners of war. By New Testament times the word referred to the release of slaves, again through the payment of a price. Exodus 21:28–32 even describes circumstances in which Jews could pay a ransom to gain release from the death penalty.

In Mark 10:45 Jesus says, "For even the Son of Man did not come to be served, but to serve, and to give his life *as a ransom* for many." Mark's allusion to a ransom payment is appropriate, for without Christ men and women are held captive and enslaved to the world, the flesh, and the devil.

Scripture is rich with redemption language. Hebrews 2:14–15 relates the death of Christ to the destruction of the devil and the release of his slaves. Jesus is spoken of as our Savior or Deliverer twenty-three times, and our deliverance is described as both a future event—from final judgment (Rom. 5:9)—and a past reality—from our state of spiritual death (Eph. 2:5, 8).

Redemption tells us two important truths about the cross. First, our salvation comes at a great cost; it took an eternal sacrifice to redeem us. Second, we have been set free to be children of God and to serve him. Whereas once we were enslaved to sin, we may now choose to serve righteousness.

Reconciliation

The work of the cross is a work of reconciliation. 2 Corinthians 5:17–18 says, ". . . if anyone is in Christ, he is a new creation; the old has gone, the new has come! All this is from God, *who reconciled us to himself through Christ.*" The Greek word translated "reconciled" in this passage indicates the changing of hostility to friendship. Because of the cross, we may now be friends with God; he reconciles us to himself.

Reconciliation is something done for us; we can take no credit for it. In Romans 5:10 Paul says that we were once "God's enemies" but now are "reconciled to him through the death of his Son." Paul says that we were reconciled when God forgave our sin by nailing it to the cross, and by "disarm[ing] the powers and authorities," which are evil spirits (Col. 2:14–15). "God demonstrates his own love for us in this," Paul says. "While we were still sinners, Christ died for us" (Rom. 5:8). In the cross God reaches out to his enemies—namely, us—and removes the barrier created by sin.

Brothers and Sisters

Not only are we reconciled to God, we are reconciled to *each other.* "His purpose was to create in himself one new man out of the two [Jew and Gentile], thus making peace, and in this one body to reconcile both of them to God through the cross, by which he put to death their hostility" (Eph. 2:15–16).

The Greek word translated "new" (*kainos*) means new in quality, in the sense of bringing into existence something that never existed in kind before. God makes us a new race of men and women. Galatians 3:28 says, "There is neither Jew nor Greek, slave nor free, male nor female, for you are all one in Christ Jesus" (see also Col. 3:11). Clearly Paul is not saying that in Christ human differences are removed; rather he says that all people have free access to God. Human inequality, so far as redemption and the kingdom of God are concerned, is abolished. God's peace is freely available to all men and women.

I know a pastor from the South whose story illustrates how the cross brings reconciliation among Christians. In November 1986 a member of his congregation gave a prophecy warning that difficult times were coming in the church and in the pastor's life. He also added this: "When the fire comes, run toward the flame, not away. Run to the hottest part and stay there as long as you can, until it kills everything that will die."

The pastor was not sure what the prophecy meant, but he took it to heart. On the first Sunday in December, at 8:55 in the morning, his assistant pastor walked into his office and announced his resignation and the establishment of a new church. The new congregation was scheduled to meet at 11:00 that very morning. More than a hundred people—almost half the congregation—left my friend's church and followed the rebellious assistant pastor. He knew immediately that this was the fire that he had been warned about earlier.

When the pastor prayed about what he should do, the Lord told him to bless those who had left. He invited his former assistant pastor back for a Sunday evening service to tell about the new church. As a result more people left. By the end of December he had lost all 11 of his key lay leaders, his worship leader, and 150 members.

I was communicating regularly with my friend during this time. I encouraged him and his wife to pray that God would bring reconciliation with those who had left. They prayed in earnest. By March 1987 all eleven of his former lay leaders had returned, asking him for forgiveness. Many of his former members returned to his congregation. Even the former assistant pastor, whose new church had fallen apart, asked him for forgiveness for dividing the church and hurting so many people. Today my friend's church is stronger and healthier than it was before the split, a living testimony to the ministry of reconciliation.

Creation

Reconciliation also extends to the entire creation. Colossians 1:19–20 says, "God was pleased . . . through him [Jesus] to reconcile to himself all things, whether things on earth or things in heaven, by making peace through his blood, shed on the cross." When Adam and Eve sinned, disorder entered creation (Rom. 5:18–19). The cross makes harmony possible in the physical and spiritual worlds—though its full realization will come only when Christ returns (Rom. 8:21).

This does not mean that by his death Christ saves *all* people. Universalism—the idea that all people will ultimately be saved—is not scriptural. The Bible speaks of an eternal hell and makes it clear that only believers in Christ are saved from eternal damnation. Forgiveness through Christ's atoning sacrifice must be received by faith. The call to all men and women is to be reconciled to God by laying aside our hostility, receiving his grace by faith, and submitting to him. The choice is ours.

The cross was also the place where Satan was defeated, which is the topic of the next chapter.

22

Recovering Lost Ground

Why is there evil in the world? Martyn Lloyd-Jones writes, "According to the Bible, the whole trouble with the world was initiated by this one who is called the devil."[1]

Scripture clearly teaches the existence and influence of Satan. "The god of this age," Paul writes, referring to the devil, "has blinded the minds of unbelievers, so that they cannot see the light of the gospel of the glory of Christ" (2 Cor. 4:4). John writes, "We know that we are children of God, and that the whole world is under the control of the evil one" (1 John 5:19). Scripture offers few explicit details about Satan, though it appears that he was at one time an angel who rebelled against God and persuaded other angels to rebel with him.

What is clear is that Satan hates God and will do anything to oppose him. He is committed to ruining God's creation and bringing down every man and woman with him. Our problem is that long ago, in the Garden of Eden, our first parents listened to Satan's lies. As a result, sin entered the world and we became Satan's slaves.

The history of humanity is colored by the murderous power of the devil, whose lust for death and evil can never be satisfied.

But the Father sent Jesus to destroy the kingdom of Satan and its evil works (John 12:31; 1 John 3:8). For God to reconcile all things to himself, Jesus had to defeat Satan and his cohorts.

Satan thought he had defeated God when he nailed Jesus to the cross. But in fact it was the Father's plan to defeat *him* through the cross. When Jesus was raised from the dead he became the first of a new race of men and women—the body of Christ, God's chosen people, a holy nation—who no longer have to be enslaved to Satan and who will eventually crush Satan under their feet (Rom. 16:20). The earth has regained its rightful Ruler and King, though the final destruction of Satan must await the return of Christ (Matt. 13:36–43).

Colossians 2:15 says, "And having disarmed the powers and authorities, he made a public spectacle of them, triumphing over them by the cross." The "powers and authorities" are evil angels. The metaphor is of a Roman general leading his captives through the streets of his city for all the citizens to see, as evidence of his victory.

In 2 Corinthians 2:14 Paul includes us in this metaphor: "But thanks be to God, who always leads us in triumphal procession in Christ . . ." Here again Paul alludes to the procession of a victorious Roman general. We are included with Christ in his triumphal procession, but not as defeated enemies. We are the triumphant warriors, men and women who have fought the good fight and won.

We enter the victorious procession of the cross through faith in Jesus (Eph. 2:8–10). This is why Satan uses any means at his disposal to blind the minds of unbelievers and to prevent them from knowing of Jesus' triumph on the cross. He does not want us to know that Jesus has defeated him.

The cross is an incredible symbol of victory over Satan, a power point that lifts us from the realm of evil and into the kingdom of God. God's power comes to us as we know and experience our justification and regeneration.

Justification

Justification is a legal term meaning "to acquit" or "to declare righteous." It is the opposite of condemnation. Justification refers to God's righteousness being credited to us. Paul says, "Consider Abraham: 'He believed God, and it was credited to him as righteousness'" (Gal. 3:6). Elsewhere he says, "God made him [Jesus] who had no sin to be sin for us, so that in him we might become the righteousness of God" (2 Cor. 5:21). When we put our faith in Christ (see Acts 10:43) we become so closely identified with him that his righteousness is credited to us, and we are declared righteous.

This is because, rather than looking at our deeds, which are evil, God, when he looks at us, sees the blood. Romans 5:9 says that we have been "justified by his [Jesus'] blood." In Romans 6:1–10, Paul says God can declare us righteous because, through faith in Christ, we have died to sin. "Anyone who has died," he argues in Romans 6:7, "has been freed from sin." The Greek word translated "freed" in this verse is the word for "justified." If by faith we identify with the cross, we are justified from sin and declared righteous.

Regeneration

Several years ago a new Christian asked me about some changes that had come into his life since he had been converted. For years he had dropped by the same bar every day after work, more for friendship than for beer. The Monday after his conversion he walked in as usual and his friends asked, "How's it going?" He ordered a beer and proceeded to tell them about how he had given his life to Christ. Suddenly his friends lapsed into a stony silence. He started feeling uncomfortable, out of place. Over the next day or two he noticed that the cigarette smoke bothered him, the beer did not taste as good as it used to, and the coarse language was suddenly foreign to him. By midweek he realized he no longer belonged there. He wanted to know how his desires could change so quickly and radically. "That's easy," I told him. "You've been regenerated, born again. You're a new man, with a new heart and desires. You'll never enjoy the old life again."

When we look at the idea of "regeneration," we leave the legal terminology of justification and come to that of childbirth. Whereas Paul normally talks about adoption into God's family, John speaks of being "born again," born of the very seed of God: "No one who is born of God will continue to sin, because God's seed remains in him; he cannot go on sinning, because he has been born of God" (1 John 3:9). When we are regenerated, our "I've-got-to-sin" nature is fundamentally changed. We are still tempted to sin, but in our hearts we want to please God.

The cross made this kind of change in me at a home Bible study group in 1963. I remember that evening as though it were last night. I did not arrive having planned to turn to Christ. Over a three-month period I had learned a lot *about* Christ and the cross—I could have passed an elementary exam on the atonement. But I did not understand that I was a sinner. I thought I was a good guy. Oh, I knew I had messed up here and there, but I did not realize how serious my condition was.

Then, suddenly, when I was least expecting it, Carol went off the deep end. She announced to the leader, Gunner Payne, "I think it's time to do something about all these things we've been talking about." The next thing I knew, she was kneeling on the floor and, as far as I could see, praying to the ceiling, weeping and telling it how sorry she was for all of her sins.

I just sat there and stared at her. "This is weird," I thought. "Why is she doing this? What has she done that's so awful? Has she done something I don't know about?" I could feel her pain and the depth of her prayers. Soon she was weeping and sobbing repeatedly, "I'm sorry for my sin."

There were six or seven people in the room, all with their eyes closed. I looked around at them. Then it hit me: *"They've all prayed this prayer, too!"* As a musician, I had been on stage enough to know when it was about to be my turn. And it was my turn now. I started sweating bullets. I thought I was going to die. The perspiration ran down my face, and I thought, "I'm not going to do this. This is dumb. I'm a good guy. I've got to get out of here."

Then it struck me. Carol was not praying to the plaster; she was praying to a *Person,* to a God who could hear her. In comparison to him, she knew she was a sinner and in need of forgiveness.

In a flash the cross made personal sense to me. Suddenly I knew something that I had never known before: I had hurt God's feelings. He loved me, and in his love for me he sent Jesus. But I had turned away from that love; I had shunned it all of my life. I was a sinner, desperately in need of the cross.

To this day I cannot fully account for how I got out of that chair. All I know is that I ended up on the floor, sobbing, nose running, eyes watering, every square inch of my flesh perspiring profusely. I had this overwhelming sense that I was talking with Someone who had been with me all of my life, but whom I had failed to recognize. Like Carol, I began talking to the living God, telling him that I was sinner. I was trying to pray the "Sinner's Prayer," but all I could do was to blub the Sinner's Blub: "Oh God! Oh God! Oh God!"

I knew something revolutionary was going on inside me. I thought, "I hope this works, because I'm making a complete fool of myself." Then the Lord brought to mind a man I had seen in Los Angeles a number of years before. He was wearing a sign that said, "I'm a fool for Christ. Whose fool are you?" I thought at the time, "That's the most stupid thing I've ever seen." But as I knelt on the floor I realized the truth of the odd sign: the cross is foolishness "to those who are perishing" (1 Cor. 1:18). That night I knelt at the cross and believed in Jesus. I have been a fool for Christ ever since.

23

Sacrificial Living

Sacrifice is at the very core of God's nature: out of love for us the Father sacrificed his only Son; out of obedience to his Father, the Son denied himself and gave his life up for us; the Holy Spirit deflects attention from himself and glorifies the Father and the Son in us.

The Bible has much to say about sacrificial living as it relates to you and me. Jesus told the disciples, "If anyone would come after me, he must deny himself and take up his cross and follow me" (Matt. 16:24). He then said that "whoever loses his life for me will find it" (16:25). Paul, echoing Christ's words, says, "I urge you, brothers, in view of God's mercy, to offer your bodies as living sacrifices, holy and pleasing to God" (Rom. 12:1). Our whole lives are meant to be a sacrifice to the Lord.

The Pearl

I was introduced to the principle of Christian sacrifice at Gunner Payne's Bible study, before I became a Christian. I can still remember the night when I first heard the parable of the pearl. Carol and Gunner were talking on and on about some issue, and I was sitting there bored, not really paying much attention. Then Gunner read

117

the passage about the pearl in the Gospel of Matthew and explained how it referred to our need to be willing to sacrifice everything in our lives for the kingdom: "the kingdom of heaven is like a merchant looking for fine pearls. When he found one of great value, he went away and sold everything he had and bought it" (Matt. 13:45–46).

That got my attention.

"Hold on a second!" I interrupted. "Are you saying that in order to become a Christian somebody might have to give up everything he has?"

"Well, what do *you* think the text means?" Gunner replied.

"I'm not sure," I said. "It *sounds* like it might mean that, but . . ." It took me a moment to collect my thoughts. "Well, I know a guy who is a musician. He doesn't know how to do anything except play music. I mean, this guy can't even tie his own shoelaces. Are you saying he might have to give up his career in order to become a Christian? How else could he make a living?"

"Your friend would have to work that out for himself," Gunner said—knowing, of course, that we were really talking about me. "But, in my opinion, he has to be *ready* to give up his career, because it's a possibility."

As I sat there thinking about what Gunner—and the Bible—appeared to be saying, two words seemed to flash across my mind: *No way.* I was at the threshold of musical success. The group I was with had records in the Top Ten. "This is crazy!" I thought. "I'm finally a success. And I'm about to make a *lot* of money. No way am I going to just give it all up."

During the next few days I was miserable, kicking and cursing and swearing around the house. In the Bible study group I had been learning new things about God, and up to that point I had liked what I had heard and had been willing to say yes. Now I had run into something that was a real obstacle: the thought that I might have to give up everything, even my career, to go on with God.

I gradually managed to reconcile myself to the idea. But only in a theoretical way, and only for "somebody else." I was not about to do anything that radical myself. No way.

You know the rest of the story. Three weeks later I was on the floor, kneeling and weeping. I had a sudden conviction that I had hurt God's feelings, and I was so sorry. When I got up off the floor, I knew I had found the Pearl of great value. And I was so glad to have it, I did not care what God wanted to take from me in return.

Sure enough, over the next few weeks God began to help me liquidate my assets. I prayed, "Okay, Lord, you can have my career," and it was as though two giant hands came out of heaven and opened my fingers, and a voice said, "Thank you."

I said goodbye to my music friends and decided to get a regular job. Suddenly I was plunged into the real world, where alarm clocks go off, where people get up and go to work in broad daylight. I had never done this. In a matter of weeks I was working in a factory, clocking on and learning how to relate to normal people.

One day I was assigned to clean some oil drums behind the factory. It was hot, filthy, smelly work. It was the most menial task they had, and the reason they had me doing it was that it was just about the only thing I *could* do.

I was down inside one of the oil drums when I heard a car drive up. A familiar voice said, "Where's John Wimber's office?" Reluctantly I came out. There stood one of my old partners from the music business. In his hand was a contract I had signed that was worth a lot of money. In order for him to fulfill it, I had to relinquish my part of it.

He just stood there staring at me. I was a mess. I had grease all over me: my hands, my clothes, my face, my hair. Finally he said, "What are you *doing* here?"

I looked at him, and then I looked at myself, then I looked at him again, then at myself. I could see myself as I must have looked to his eyes.

Right at that moment, I did not particularly feel like I had the Pearl. I could not think of a single thing to say. After a long silence I answered lamely, "God did this to me."

His eyes narrowed with a look of resolve, as if to say, "He's never going to do it to me."

I felt ashamed. Obviously what I was doing with my life seemed to be utter foolishness to him. At that moment I could not think of a single persuasive explanation for why God—this God of love, this God that is so great in the Bible, this God that is so nice to so many people—was apparently being so mean to me. Why *had* he chosen to treat me this way?

As I watched my friend drive away, I realized that sometimes there is no way to explain obedience and sacrifice to God to those who do not see the Pearl. My friend could not see any value at all in the humiliation of my flesh, in God taking me down from my lofty, worldly position and teaching me simple obedience.

Since that day I have found that all through our lives, in our service to God and his people, we will be put in situations where others will look at us with disdain because our obedience and sacrifice to God does not make sense to them. But for those of us who have found the Pearl, it all makes perfect sense. We know that it is worth everything to follow him, to walk with him, to serve him, to lose our lives for him. It is worth selling everything we own in order to gain Christ and be found in him.

Sacrifice

Sacrifice should not be thought of primarily in negative terms. The greatest of all Christian virtues is love (1 Cor. 13:13), and the purpose of the greatest sacrifice ever made was to release the love of God on all men and women. Sacrifice is not an end in itself; we take up our crosses in order to more fully follow Christ. I might have given up a promising career as a musician, but I gained the infinite joy of knowing God and eternal life. I thought it was a pretty good deal back in 1963, and I still think so today.[1]

Sacrifice also releases power. The greater the sacrifice, the greater the power released. The greatest of all sacrifices, the sacrifice of Jesus, has released the greatest power of all. At the very moment of his death, even before the resurrection, the natural realm could not contain the power released from the throne of heaven. The power of the cross invaded every realm of this world. It shook the foundations of the earth. It assaulted the religious realm, ripping open the temple veil from top to bottom, from heaven to earth. It even took on the greatest enemy of all, death, releasing dead and rotting bodies from their tombs (Matt. 27:51–52). This same power is available to us as we pick up our crosses daily (Matt. 16:24–25).

The relationship between sacrifice and power is illustrated in Christian *martyrdom*. The death of Stephen, for instance, precipitated a release of heavenly power that led to revival and the conversion of Paul (Acts 7:57–8:3).

Christian martyrdom is not confined to ancient church history. According to David Barrett, the editor of the *World Christian Encyclopedia,* on average 300,000 Christians have been martyred each year in the twentieth century.[2] Some of the readers of this book may even be called by God to martyrdom, for great sacrifice accompanies the release of God's love and power.

Martyrdom is far from being the only form of sacrifice that releases God's love and power. Excepting martyrdom, the highest form of sacrifice is *celibacy,* forgoing the joy and security of marriage and family in order to be a special companion to Jesus. Jesus spoke of those who made themselves eunuchs for the kingdom of God (Matt. 19:12), and Isaiah said that faithful eunuchs would have in God's temple "a memorial and a name better than [that of] sons and daughters" (Isa. 56:5). A person who is gifted and called to a life of celibacy is free from the normal distractions of marriage and family; he or she can be totally devoted to the things of the Lord (1 Cor. 7:32–35).

For those of us who are not called to celibacy, God has provided other means of sacrifice. At the top of the list stands *prayer* and *fasting*. The power released by prayer is truly amazing. Prayer is the instrument that God will use to open or shut the heavens (James 5:16–18). When prayer is combined with fasting, whole armies can be defeated (1 Sam. 7:6–13; 2 Chron. 20:1–30). Even the judgment of God on evil people can be turned back through prayer and fasting (1 Kings 21:27–29; Jonah 3:5–10); and through it the power of the devil and his demons is overcome (Matt. 4:1–11; Mark 9:29, AV).

Finally, *giving money and material possessions to the poor and to God's work* is a powerful form of sacrifice. Giving that is motivated by love for God and his purposes releases great power and secures blessing (Phil. 4:18–19). The centurion Cornelius "gave generously to those in need and prayed to God regularly," which caught the Lord's attention (Acts 10:2). An angel appeared to Cornelius in a vision, commended him for his generosity and prayer life, and directed him to contact Peter, which opened the gospel to the Gentiles.

One Step at a Time

From time to time the Lord challenges us to make new commitments. He lets us know that he wants us to give up something we are successful at and begin doing something we do not yet know anything about—maybe something we do not even like.

The simple fact of the matter is that the Lord has the right to call us to make any changes and sacrifices he wants, since he has purchased us at the price of his own blood. But when he exercises that right, we often go into a tailspin. "Who does he think he *is?*" we protest. "I've just got my life where I want it, I'm just going in the direction I want to go, and now he's telling me I have to do something different."

What do we do? Do we back off, take a vacation from obedience and sacrifice, and do our own thing? Do we try to hang on to Jesus while brushing away the cross? Or do we say yes to Jesus and no to our desires—and release the power of God in our lives?

The economy of the kingdom of God is quite simple. Every new step in the kingdom costs us everything we have gained to date. Every time we come to cross a new threshold, it costs us everything we now have. Every new step may cost us all the reputation and security we have accumulated up to that point. It costs us our life.

A disciple is always ready to take the next step. If there is anything that characterizes Christian maturity, it is the willingness to become a beginner again for Jesus Christ. It is the willingness to put our hand in his hand and say, "I'm scared to death, but I'll go with you. You're the Pearl of great price."

PART VII

Depending on
the Holy Spirit

24

Introducing the Holy Spirit

Of the three Persons of the Trinity, the Holy Spirit raises the most puzzling questions. Who is he? How can we experience him? What does it mean to be filled with the Holy Spirit? How does he guide us? What are spiritual gifts? Christians disagree on some of these questions, though I believe there are some biblical answers on which we can agree.

Who Is He?

Before we can correctly understand the *work* of the Holy Spirit in spiritual growth, we must get to know him. "A frequent source of error and fanaticism about the work of the Holy Spirit," writes R. A. Torrey, "is the attempt to study and understand His work without first coming to know Him as a person."[1]

Some people think of the Holy Spirit as an ethereal force—an "it"—that produces warm and loving feelings. But the Holy Spirit is a person. A masculine pronoun (*ekeinos*) is used of him in the Greek New Testament, even though the Greek noun for "Spirit" (*pneuma*) is neuter (John 14:17; 15:26; 16:14). Jesus and the writers of the New Testament called the Spirit "he" (see John 14:17). The Holy

Spirit has intelligence (John 14:26; Rom. 8:16), will (Acts 16:7; 1 Cor. 12:11), and emotions (Isa. 63:10; Eph. 4:30). He is spoken of as a divine Person in relation to the Son and Father (2 Cor. 13:14; 1 Pet. 1:2), and he manifested himself as a person distinct from the Son and Father (Matt. 3:16–17).

The significance of this is that we can know the Holy Spirit *personally*; not just as an impersonal influence, a good feeling, or a "spark of God in all of us." He is called a "paraclete" (*parakletos*)—translated "counselor," "instructor," "helper," or "advocate" (see John 14:16; 15:26; 16:7; 1 John 2:1). Jesus said, "I will ask the Father, and he will give you another Counselor to be with you forever—the Spirit of truth" (John 14:16–17). In other words, the Holy Spirit is a personal friend of God's people (Acts 15:28).

The Holy Spirit is also God. He is called the "*Holy* Spirit" (Luke 11:13) and the "Spirit of God" (Rom. 8:14). In Acts 5:3–4, Peter accuses Ananias of lying to the Holy Spirit, then says, "You have not lied to men but to God"—showing that Peter regarded the Holy Spirit as God himself present with his people. The Spirit possesses attributes that the other members of the Trinity possess, such as life (Rom. 8:2), truth (John 16:13), love (Rom. 15:30), holiness (Eph. 4:30), eternity (Heb. 9:14), omnipresence (Ps. 139:7), and omniscience (Rom. 8:27).

Fingerprints of God

Of the members of the Trinity, the Holy Spirit is actually the closest to us, giving life to our bodies and dwelling personally in our hearts (John 14:17b). However, it is a bit more difficult to understand the Holy Spirit's personality. This is because the Holy Spirit aims only to promote the glory of Christ and draws no attention to himself. Jesus said: "He [the Spirit] will bring glory to me by taking from what is mine and making it known to you. All that belongs to the Father is mine. That is why I said the Spirit will take from what is mine and make it known to you" (John 16:14–15).

Because he is always pointing us toward Jesus, much of our knowledge of the Holy Spirit is indirect, drawn from the fingerprints of his presence in creation and in our lives. Here are some things the Spirit has done and does for us.

1. *He helped in the creation.* In the creation, Genesis says, the "Spirit of God was hovering over the waters" (Gen. 1:2).

2. *He gives and sustains life.* In the Old Testament the word Spirit (Hebrew *ruach*) could also mean "breath," which was symbolic of life itself (Gen. 2:7; 6:3; see also Ezek. 37:10). John 6:63 says, "The Spirit gives life" (see also 2 Cor. 3:6).

3. *He convicts us of sin, righteousness, and judgment.* Jesus says, "When he [the Spirit] comes, he will convict the world of guilt in regard to sin . . . because men do not believe in me" (John 16:8–9; see also 1 Thess. 1:5). Only sinners recognize they need a Savior. The Spirit convicts men and women of sin, enabling them to see that they need a Savior (Rom. 2:14–15).

The Spirit also convicts us concerning Jesus' righteousness (John 16:8, 10). It is the Holy Spirit who confirms the truth of the gospel in the hearts of men and women, bearing witness that Jesus is the Christ, the Son of God. Jesus said that the Spirit "will testify about me" (John 15:26; see also 5:37; 16:14; 1 John 5:7–12). Thus the Holy Spirit verifies Jesus' claims, making the preaching of the gospel effectual in those who believe, by inwardly testifying to the reality of Christ and to the truth of the word of God (1 Thess. 1:5–6).

Finally, the Holy Spirit convicts us concerning judgment (John 16:11). If we reject the double conviction of sin and righteousness, he reminds us that we will surely be held accountable for our words[2] and our actions (Matt. 12:36–37; see also Matt. 25:41; Rom. 3:19).

4. *He attracts us to Jesus.* He testifies about Jesus and glorifies him (John 15:26; 16:14). Even though it took weeks for me to put my faith in Christ, I could not stay away from Gunner Payne's Bible study group. There was something in me that kept drawing me back

to the Bible study and gave me a desire to learn more about Jesus. It was like a voice is my heart that kept whispering, "Yes. This is all true. Jesus is all that he claimed to be." The Holy Spirit was already at work in my heart, drawing me toward Jesus.

5. *He gives us new life.* It is the Spirit who gives us new life, a new nature, making us new creatures who are no longer in bondage to sin (Gal. 5:16). This is called "regeneration," or being born again: "I tell you the truth, no one can enter the kingdom of God unless he is born of water and the Spirit. Flesh gives birth to flesh, but the Spirit gives birth to spirit" (John 3:5–6).

6. *He dwells within us.* Speaking to the disciples, Jesus said, "But you know him [the Holy Spirit], for he lives with you and will be in you" (John 14:17). The result of this indwelling is a "mystical union" with Christ himself. Though Christ is seated at the right hand of the Father (Eph. 1:20) and we are on earth and not yet with him (Phil. 1:23), through the agency of the Spirit there is a union with Christ. And he assures us of his redemption (Eph. 1:13–14).

7. *He enables us to experience our adoption as God's children.* Romans 8:15 says, "For you did not receive a spirit that makes you a slave again to fear, but you received the Spirit of sonship. And by him we cry, '*Abba,* Father'" (see also Gal. 4:6; 1 John 3:1). Our adoption means we can experience the Father intimately. "The Spirit himself testifies with our spirit that we are God's children" (Rom. 8:16).

8. *He prays in and through us.* He intercedes "with groans that words cannot express" when we do not know how to pray (Rom. 8:26). This is part and parcel with Christ's intercession for us (Rom. 8:34; Heb. 7:25).

9. *He gives spiritual gifts to the church.* It is the same Spirit who is the source of all the gifts. We should seek the gifts for the common good of the body of Christ (1 Cor. 12:7). An excellent guide for the godly operation of the gifts appears in 1 Corinthians 12–14. I will take a closer look at the distribution and use of gifts in Chapters 28 and 29.

10. *He makes us one.* Paul writes, "For we were all baptized by one Spirit into one body—whether Jews or Greeks, slave or free—and we were all given the one Spirit to drink" (1 Cor. 12:13; see also Eph. 2:18; 4:3–4; Phil. 2:1).

11. *He illumines our minds.* Jesus says, "But when . . . the Spirit of truth comes, he will guide you into all truth" (John 16:13). He does this for us both individually and for the church as a whole (Acts 8:29, 39; 13:1–3; 21:4).

12. *He provides resurrection power.* The Father used the Spirit to raise Jesus from the dead (Rom. 8:11). The Spirit will likewise raise us up and give us "spiritual" bodies (1 Cor. 15:44–45). He will sustain our lives at the resurrection, giving us eternal life (2 Cor. 4:14; 1 Pet. 3:18; 4:6; Rev. 11:11).

13. *He empowers and guides us in our witness and service.* In Acts 4 the Spirit gave the apostles boldness to continue proclaiming the gospel (Acts 4:31; see also 1 Thess. 1:5). When we teach and preach in the power of the Holy Spirit, he guides our words so as to minister to those who hear. Furthermore, he gives us power to do the works of Jesus—healings, deliverance, even miracles (Acts 1:8; Rom. 15:19; 1 Cor. 2:4).

14. *He produces spiritual growth.* Jesus sanctifies us through the Holy Spirit: ". . . you were washed, you were sanctified, you were justified in the name of the Lord Jesus Christ and by the Spirit of our God" (1 Cor. 6:11; see also Rom. 15:16; 2 Thess. 2:13). *How* the Spirit produces growth—and our part in cooperating with him in that process—is the topic of the next two chapters.

25

Depending on the Holy Spirit

When I speak to Christian groups about the Holy Spirit I usually introduce the topic by asking a question: "How do you maintain a right relationship with God?" Their answers vary greatly:

"Believe right theology."

"Obey all the rules, especially the Ten Commandmants."

"*Resolve* to obey all the rules, especially those emphasized in our particular church."

"Attend the right church every week."

"Memorize Scripture."

"Take Communion regularly."

"Witness to at least one person every day."

And so on.

These are, of course, all activities that should mark our lives. After all, who could object to regular church attendance, good theology, and obedience to God's word? In fact, I do not object to these virtuous acts. But I do object to their being made the basis for initiating and maintaining our relationship with God. This assumption leads to the illusion that we *earn* right standing with God by *doing* the right things.

If ever there were a man who could cite spiritual accomplishments as a basis for knowing God, it was Paul. Yet Paul did not see it that way. He said, "By the grace of God I am what I am" (1 Cor. 15:10; see also Phil. 3:4–9). For Paul, good works were clearly the *result,* not the means, of a relationship with God:

> For it is by grace you have been saved, through faith—and this not from yourselves, it is the gift of God—not by works, so that no one can boast. For we are God's workmanship, *created in Christ Jesus to do good works,* which God prepared in advance for us to do. (Eph. 2:8–10)

Good works are not the *means* by which we maintain our relationship with God; they are the *result* of dependence on the Holy Spirit. But there is something in all of us that resists dependence on anything other than ourselves. All our lives we have been trained and conditioned to believe in ourselves, to rely on our own wisdom, our own strength. Before we can say in our hearts, "Come Holy Spirit, and do with me as you please," we must first say, "O God, I cannot do a thing." Then God says, "Okay. Now we can have a relationship."

Moses

Moses is an outstanding example of one dependent on God. Scripture says, "Now Moses was a very humble man, more humble than anyone else on the face of the earth" (Num. 12:3).

But he was not always that way. When Moses was forty years old he attempted to serve God in his own strength. One day in Egypt he saw a Jewish slave being mistreated, so he courageously went to his aid and killed the abusive Egyptian. But he was discovered, and he fled to the desert. Moses had given God his best effort and failed. For the next forty years he lived in obscurity.

Moses was so thoroughly broken that when at the burning bush God called him to be Israel's ruler and deliverer (Acts 7:35), he responded with reluctance. God answered, "I will be with you" (Exod. 3:12). Moses next asked God, "What if they [the Israelites] don't believe me?" (4:1)—this despite God's assurances that he would be with him! God answered by performing signs and wonders through Moses; they were given to authenticate Moses' ministry (4:2–9). Furthermore, Moses doubted his ability to speak adequately: "I am slow of speech and tongue" (4:10). God reminded Moses that he (the Lord) gave him a mouth, and he promised to help him speak (4:11–12). Yet Moses remained unconvinced. "O Lord," he pleaded, "please send someone else" (4:13). This response tested the Lord's patience, but he graciously provided Aaron to go alongside and speak for Moses (4:14–17).

Only when we come to a point where we totally abandon any confidence we have had in our own strength, gifts, and talents, are we fit vessels for the Holy Spirit. Only when we come to a point of complete and continuing dependence on God—"Lord, I can do nothing to advance your kingdom"—can we know the fullness of the Holy Spirit.

God was patient with Moses because he knew that his responses were rooted in dependence on him. Moses was fit to be filled with God's glory, because any sense of self-reliance was drained from him.

In the Old Testament the Holy Spirit only came temporarily on special people for special tasks. Moses lamented, "I wish that all the Lord's people were prophets and that the Lord would put his Spirit on them!" (Num. 11:29). But it was not to be under the old covenant.

A Better Covenant

The prophet Jeremiah, however, saw better days coming:

> "The time is coming," declares the Lord, "when I will make a new covenant with the house of Israel and with the house of Judah. It

will not be like the covenant I made with their forefathers when I took them by the hand to lead them out of Egypt. . . . I will put my law in their minds and write it on their hearts." (Jer. 31:31–33)

And how would God write his law on his people's hearts? Joel prophesied that Moses' wish would be fulfilled:

And afterward, I will pour out my Spirit on all people. Your sons and daughters will prophesy, your old men will dream dreams, your young men will see visions. Even on my servants, both men and women, I will pour out my Spirit in those days. (Joel 2:28–29)

Jesus introduced a covenant better than Moses'—a covenant of grace in which the Holy Spirit is freely and fully available to all who come to the Father through Jesus (2 Cor. 3:3, 7–8).

Under the new covenant the ministry of the Holy Spirit is for everyone—young and old, male and female, leaders and rank-and-file members. But how does the Holy Spirit come to us? And what do we have to do to experience his presence in our lives? That is the topic of the next chapter.

26

Baptized in the Holy Spirit

We often hear people speak of being "baptized in the Holy Spirit." What does this phrase mean?

We first hear of being baptized in the Holy Spirit from John the Baptist: "I baptize you with water. But one more powerful than I will come, the thongs of whose sandals I am not worthy to untie. He will baptize you with the Holy Spirit and with fire" (Luke 3:16; see also Matt. 3:11; Mark 1:8). Later, at Christ's baptism, John proclaimed, ". . . the one who sent me to baptize with water told me, 'The man on whom you see the Spirit come down and remain is he who will baptize with the Holy Spirit.' I have seen and I testify that this [Jesus] is the Son of God" (John 1:33–34).

John contrasted his own baptizing with the Messiah's, which would come at a future, undisclosed time. John's baptizing was with water; the Messiah's was with the Holy Spirit.

After his resurrection Jesus reminded the disciples of John's teaching when he said, "John baptized with water, but in a few days you will be baptized with the Holy Spirit" (Acts 1:5). At Pentecost Jesus' words were fulfilled:

> Suddenly a sound like the blowing of a violent wind came from
> heaven and filled the whole house where they were sitting. They
> saw what seemed to be tongues of fire that separated and came to

rest on each of them. All of them were filled with the Holy Spirit
and began to speak in other tongues as the Spirit enabled them.
(Acts 2:2–4)

Luke describes Pentecost as a filling with the Holy Spirit, and
Peter in his address to a crowd proclaims they are witnessing the
fulfillment of Joel's prophecy:

"'In the last days, God says,
  I will pour out my Spirit on all
    people.
Your sons and daughters will
    prophesy,
  your young men will see visions,
  your old men will dream dreams.
Even on my servants, both men and
    women,
  I will pour out my Spirit in those
    days,
  and they will prophesy.'" (Acts 2:17–18; Joel 2:28–29)

Later the Holy Spirit fell on a group of Gentiles gathered in Cornelius' house (Acts 10:44–46). They too spoke in tongues and
praised God.

"To baptize" in Greek can mean "to dip" or "to immerse." It con-
veys the sense of being overwhelmed. John the Baptist, Jesus, and
Peter all taught that we should expect to be immersed in—overwhelmed by—the Holy Spirit, and that this baptism is essential for
true discipleship. What exactly does being baptized in the Holy
Spirit accomplish?

First Corinthians 12:13 is probably the most relevant verse in the
Bible on this topic: "For we were all baptized by one Spirit into one
body—whether Jews or Greeks, slave or free—and we were all given
the one Spirit to drink." Here Paul teaches that Jesus baptizes us
with the Holy Spirit for, among other things, the purpose of incor-
poration into the body of Christ. John R. W. Stott comments,

Depending on the Holy Spirit

"So the baptism of the Spirit in this verse, far from being a dividing factor (some have it, others have not), is the great uniting factor (an experience we have all had)."[1]

How do we experience Spirit baptism? It comes at conversion. Scripture teaches, "no one can say, 'Jesus is Lord,' except by the Holy Spirit" (1 Cor. 12:3), and "if anyone does not have the Spirit of Christ, he does not belong to Christ" (Rom. 8:9). Conversion and Holy Spirit baptism are simultaneous experiences. The born-again experience is the consummate charismatic experience.

Filled with the Spirit

If we are in Christ, the Holy Spirit is in us. Having the Holy Spirit, however, does not guarantee that we will experience his power and gifts. More is required of us for that to happen. Paul even *commands* us to be filled with the Spirit: "Do not get drunk on wine, which leads to debauchery. Instead, be filled with the Spirit" (Eph. 5:18). He contrasts pagan gatherings, marked by drunkenness and debauchery, with those of Spirit-filled Christians, who "speak to one another with psalms, hymns and spiritual songs . . . [and give] thanks to God the Father for everything" (Eph. 5:19–20).

There is a problem with being too precise about the terms "filling," "filled," and "being full," because Paul and Luke use them differently. Paul refers to any ensuing interaction between the individual and the Holy Spirit following our initial baptism as a filling. Luke, however, seems to use the term filling in a less settled manner. He employs three Greek words for filling, and they all give a slightly different twist to its meaning.

First, Acts 6:5 describes filling more like a *character quality* or disposition in which a person is habitually controlled by God's Spirit. "They chose Stephen, a man full [*plērēs*] of faith and of the Holy Spirit" (see also Luke 4:1; Acts 6:3; 11:24). In this passage, to be "full of the Holy Spirit" is synonymous with possessing mature character.

Second, Acts 2:4 emphasizes the *sovereign and initiatory anointing* of the Holy Spirit: "All of them were filled [*pimplēmi*] with the Holy

Spirit and began to speak in other tongues as the Spirit enabled them" (see also Luke 1:15, 41, 67; Acts 4:8, 31; 7:55; 9:17; 13:9). Note that in these verses being "filled" is akin to Paul's being "baptized by one Spirit" in 1 Corinthians 12:13. These fillings are sudden and dramatic, yet they have no discernible pattern of results. They might be accompanied by tongues speaking, preaching, or—as John the Baptist did—leaping in the womb! (Luke 1:41).

Finally, in Acts 13:52 the disciples' filling comes as a *result* of their bold preaching of the word of God: "And the disciples were filled [*plēroō*] with joy and with the Holy Spirit." Like the previous category, this is a sudden filling.

From Luke we can draw two conclusions regarding the filling of the Holy Spirit. First, unlike Paul, Luke does not command us to be filled with the Spirit. There is almost an assumption in Luke that as you seek God and walk in obedience with him the Holy Spirit will fill you. Your character will be marked by the Spirit's presence, and he will send special anointings on you as you minister.

Second, God frequently and sovereignly fills his servants with the Spirit, as he did in Acts 7:55 when Stephen saw Jesus in heaven, standing at the Father's side. These sovereign anointings are usually associated with special service, especially witnessing, as when Peter preached with boldness before the Sanhedrin in Acts 4.

There is in Scripture no discernible pattern or formula for how the Spirit falls on us. But we should not be surprised by this, because Jesus said, "The wind blows wherever it pleases. You hear its sound, but you cannot tell where it comes from or where it is going. So it is with everyone born of the Spirit" (John 3:8).

What Must I Do?

We are not left completely in the dark, however, about how to experience the Holy Spirit. After all, in Ephesians 5:18 Paul did command us to be filled with the Spirit. Incidentally, the Greek word that Paul uses there is the same word Luke used in Acts 13:52, in which the filling came as a result of the disciples' steadfast faithfulness to the gospel. Paul instructs the Ephesians earlier in the chapter to understand and do the Lord's will (v. 17), implying that as they do so they will be filled with the Spirit.

There are a number of things that we can do to cultivate a fertile *environment* for the Holy Spirit's sovereign activity in our lives. Our part is to obey; his part is to do as he pleases.

First, we must keep our *hearts clean,* for sin grieves the Holy Spirit. We do this through confession of sin: "And do not grieve the Holy Spirit of God, with whom you were sealed for the day of redemption. Get rid of all bitterness, rage and anger, brawling and slander, along with every form of malice" (Eph. 4:30–31). Paul's list of sins here is only a sampling; *all* sin grieves the Spirit, for he is holy (Rom. 1:4). Through confession we maintain clean hearts that are fit to be controlled by the Holy Spirit. As we confess our conscious sins, "he is faithful and just and will forgive us our sins and purify us from all unrighteousness" (1 John 1:9).

Second, by faith we must call for the presence of the Holy Spirit, praying for him to come into our lives. 1 John 5:14 says, "This is the confidence we have in approaching God: that if we ask anything according to his will, he hears us." We already know that his will is that we be filled with the Spirit (Eph. 5:18), so we can with great confidence pray, "Come, Holy Spirit, and fill our lives."

Third, we must thirst after the Holy Spirit. John 7:37 says:

> . . . Jesus stood and said in a loud voice, "If anyone is thirsty, let him come to me and drink. Whoever believes in me, as the Scripture has said, streams of living water will flow from within him." By this he meant the Spirit, whom those who believed in him were later to receive.

Jesus is calling us to a jealous thirst, one in which nothing else will satisfy the longing of our hearts.

The evangelist Dwight L. Moody captures the intensity of a thirst for God in his testimony:

> I began to cry as never before, for a greater blessing from God. The hunger increased; I really felt that I did not want to live any longer.

[He had been a Christian, and not only a Christian but a minister, and in charge of a mission for some time; he was getting conversions but still he wanted more.] I kept on crying all the time that God would fill me with his Spirit. Well, one day in the city of New York—oh! what a day, I cannot describe it, I seldom refer to it. It is almost too sacred an experience to name. Paul had an experience of which he never spoke for 14 years. I can only say, God revealed himself to me, and I had such an experience of his love that I had to ask him to stay his hand.

Commenting on Moody's experience, Martyn Lloyd-Jones writes, "That [the experience of the Holy Spirit] is what turned D. L. Moody from a good, regular, ordinary minister, into the evangelist who was so signally used of God in this and in other countries."[2] "Blessed are those who hunger and thirst for righteousness, for they will be filled" (Matt. 5:6).

Fourth, we must *walk* with the Spirit. Galatians 5:25 says, "Since we live by the Spirit, let us keep in step with the Spirit." If the Holy Spirit is the source of our lives, Paul says, then he should direct our course. This involves both knowing the word of God and cultivating a sensitivity to the still, small voice of God speaking his direction to us (John 10:4).

Finally, we must make ourselves available to the Holy Spirit through *obedience to his word*. In obedience to Jesus' instructions, the disciples gathered in Jerusalem on Pentecost and were filled with the Spirit (Acts 1:4; 2:4). Peter obeyed God and preached to the Sanhedrin in Acts 4:8, and he was filled with the Spirit. When we are where God wants us to be, doing what God wants us to do, his Spirit usually comes. When I pray for the sick I rarely at first feel the anointing of the Holy Spirit. But as I pray I frequently sense the Holy Spirit come on me, empower my prayers, and heal the sick. I start praying because Jesus commanded me to heal the sick, not because he promises perfect results.

What happens when the Spirit empowers us for service? That is the topic of the remainder of Part VII.

27

The Holy Transformer

We can rest in the knowledge that when we put our faith in Christ, he baptizes us with the Holy Spirit. The Holy Spirit is a gift of grace, bringing us into union with Jesus (John 14:20). He applies grace to our lives (Rom. 14:17). That is why in Galatians 5:22–23 the marks of true maturity—love, joy, peace, patience, kindness, goodness, faithfulness, gentleness, and self-control—are called the fruit of the *Spirit,* not the fruit of our efforts.

It is not the case, however, that we are supposed merely to sit around and wait for the Spirit to make us holy. Just the opposite is true. Scripture uses active verbs to communicate our part in spiritual growth: "So I say, *live* by the Spirit, and you will not gratify the desires of the sinful nature" (Gal. 5:16); "Since we live by the Spirit, let us *keep in step* with the Spirit" (Gal. 5:25); "As God's chosen people, holy and dearly loved, *clothe yourselves* with compassion, kindness, humility, gentleness and patience" (Col. 3:12).

Spiritual growth, then, is a product of the initiating, empowering work of the Holy Spirit *and* of our active cooperation. He engages our minds, wills, and emotions and he expects us to respond. If *either* divine initiative *or* human response is missing, we will not grow.

Let us consider three key points at which the Spirit's grace and our active cooperation can coincide: Scripture, life's circumstances, and fellowship. These are means of grace for us. The Holy Spirit works in and through them for spiritual growth.

The Word of God

The first and primary means of grace is the *word of God,* Scripture. Jesus prayed, "Sanctify them [make them holy] by the truth; your word is truth" (John 17:17). Scripture has the power to teach, introduce clear thinking, inform our consciences, conform our lives to God's standards (2 Tim. 3:16), protect us against sin (Ps. 119:11), and bring freedom (Ps. 119:45).

I devoted a great deal of space to this topic back in Part III ("Believing God's Word"), and I will not repeat what I said there. However, I would like to emphasize a point that I believe is critical for spiritual growth: We must *act on* what we learn from the word of God, or our belief and knowledge are not authentic.

The knowledge of God is progressive: we hear God's word and believe; then we act on our belief; and as a result our knowledge of God increases and we have a new opportunity for belief, action, and so on.

As a new Christian, I thought my personal pilgrimage with God was the essence of Christianity. I used to evaluate myself over and over again, asking, "Am I growing, Lord?" I remember spending days memorizing Scripture; I got up to about a thousand verses memorized. I thought, "Boy, I must really be mature. I must really be growing. Look at all these verses that I have memorized." That was how the Bible memory course motivated me: "You want to grow in Christ? Memorize his word." But I was not growing as I knew I should. I was still biting my wife's head off, yelling at my kids, and doing a thousand things that showed in my relationships that I had not grown a bit. I had lots of verses memorized but few were worked out in my life. I had to learn about putting scriptural truth into action.

141

In 1977 I became convinced that the Bible teaches we should heal the sick, and so in obedience to God I started praying for the sick every week. But nothing happened. A few weeks of fruitless prayers soon turned to several months. Still nothing. I became angry and frustrated. "I will not teach about healing anymore," I yelled at God one day. "Preach my word," he responded, "not your experience." I obeyed. *Ten months* later, a woman was healed and I experienced a vision of Jesus' healing power. Then I knew in a deeper way that Jesus is full of compassion. And I knew that in the power of the Holy Spirit I *could* heal the sick. My relationship with Jesus was radically changed through that experience, and thousands of others have been affected by what I learned. But none of that would have happened had I not been willing to take a risk and act on God's word.

Life's Circumstances

The Holy Spirit orders the circumstances of our lives so that we may grow closer to him. Romans 8:28 says, "And we know that in all things God works for the good of those who love him, who have been called according to his purpose." Things that other people—or even Satan—intend for evil, God uses for good (see Gen. 50:20), to mold our character in conformity to his Son. He allows suffering for our good when we go astray (Ps. 119:67). But we do not have to be full of sin for suffering to come into our lives. If we are identified with Jesus, we should expect his sufferings to flow over into our lives (2 Cor. 1:5).

Much of my thinking about suffering is summed up in the life of Gunner Payne, the man who led me to Christ back in 1963. The first time I met Gunner I knew there was something different about him. He was a good teacher—intelligent, insightful, patient. But what impressed me most about him was the quality of the man, a central aspect of which was his character. He appeared to be sound, complete, uncorrupted. Nothing mattered to him except living for God. What was it that created such a pervasive peace in him? I soon discovered the secret of Gunner's maturity: he had learned to trust Jesus Christ through immense personal suffering.

In 1952 a young man attacked his fifteen-year-old daughter, Ruby Ann, brutally murdering her. The ensuing trial (which dragged on for six years) drew national attention when it became a test case for capital punishment. Then, in 1962, tragedy struck again when their twenty-two-year-old son, Preston, suffered massive injuries in an automobile accident. To this day Gunner and his wife still care for Preston.

The night of Ruby Ann's death, Gunner gathered his wife and son around the table and prayed, "Father, I don't understand. But I won't question. I trust you." Gunner prayed that prayer many times since then and, I am convinced, discovered a key to understanding and growing through suffering. Through the years of pain and trust, Jesus forged mature character and dignity in Gunner. More than anything else, he was at peace with God. His spiritual peace also affected how he related to others. For example, Gunner was a peacemaker with other people. He never spoke against others, choosing instead to find the best in them. I visited him many times at his welding shop and watched him work hard to please his customers. He charged fair prices for his work and was generous with his time and money. Despite going through tragedies that would break up most marriages, Gunner loved and cared for his wife and son.

Gunner's life contains a secret about how to make the most out of suffering. He flourished spiritually in the midst of suffering because he understood the goal of the Christian life, that we might "become mature, attaining to the whole measure of the fullness of Christ" (Eph. 4:13).

When we suffer we are confronted with a choice. We can believe that God is unjust and does not care for us, or we can believe that he is good and that whatever comes from his hand is tempered with mercy and his desire for our growth. Gunner may not have understood *why* Ruby Ann had to die, but he could understand that God was in control and that God is good. Romans 1:17 says, ". . . in the gospel a righteousness from God is revealed, a righteousness that is by faith from first to last, just as it is written: 'The righteous will live by faith.'" The exercise of faith that produces righteousness includes trusting God in dire circumstances.

In Hebrews 11, the classic New Testament passage on faith, we read that "faith is being sure of what we hope for and certain of what we do not see" (v. 1). Faith is characterized by people believing God's word regardless of their circumstances. This is not "blind faith" at all, but *informed* faith, trust in a God who overcame the most evil circumstance in all of human history: the cross. Jesus, Scripture teaches, learned obedience through suffering (Heb. 5:8). If he, being sinless, had to endure suffering, how much more should we trust God in our suffering? Coming into conformity with Jesus Christ requires accepting *all* life's circumstances as coming from God's hand and cooperating with the Holy Spirit's transforming power in the midst of suffering.

Fellowship

The Greek word that is commonly translated "fellowship" implies far more than socializing at potluck suppers or chatting on the church's front lawn after Sunday services. The word means holding our lives in common, something that the first-century Christians demonstrated through spiritual, social, and material generosity toward one another. In the early church there was a relationship between the believers' warmth of heart toward God and their generosity toward one another. So close were these relationships that the early Christians did not see themselves as isolated individuals, but as "members one of another," joined together in communities where individuals experienced the Holy Spirit, grew to maturity, and cooperated with each other in advancing God's kingdom.

Within these communities they gained strength, support, and protection from the corroding influences of the world (Col. 3:16). Thus they were well prepared to face anything the devil might throw at them when they went out into the world. This quality of relationship contrasts sharply with the faith and practice of many modern Christians, who narrow their relationship with God to individualistic concerns like repentance and conversion, prayer and Scripture study, personal righteousness and evangelism. God has called us to grow to maturity *in the body of Christ*. We are called to "reach unity in the faith and in the knowledge of the Son of God," growing up "into him who is the Head, that is, Christ. From him the whole body, joined and held together by every supporting ligament, grows and builds itself up in love, as each part does its work" (Eph. 4:13, 15–16).

When we make a commitment to Christ we make a commitment to his purpose in the world, part of which is to have a healthy, unified body, the people of God. A few years ago God showed me that I had sinned many times against the body of Christ. I had become judgmental of the larger church. God spoke to me about loving the things that he loves, and *God loves his church*. He loves the *whole* church—Protestant and Catholic, Orthodox and Anabaptist. Now, by this I do not mean that he loves all the things different religious groups believe and do. Nor of course am I saying that I agree with all the beliefs of other denominations. But Jesus deeply loves his church, and we have been called to love the things that Jesus loves. So we have no choice but to love the whole church—even those parts we do not agree with.

If we love the church then we will submit to it, for it is "the pillar and foundation of the truth" (1 Tim. 3:15). There is of course great personal benefit for us when we place ourselves under the church and honor and respect its leaders. After all, the word of God is preached in the church, and God has ordained pastors to lead and protect us. The church is also a community of prayer, and spiritual growth is impossible without personal and corporate prayer.

Finally, the church is where the sacraments, baptism, and Communion, are practised. Sacraments are "visible signs of inward grace," the means to a fresh experience of our union and communion with Jesus. They point us away from ourselves and toward our foundations in Christ.

The New Testament plainly teaches that our new birth is an act of God's Spirit through God's mercy alone and is not effected by human effort or merit. Baptism communicates all that it means to be in Christ: a sharing in the death and resurrection of Jesus, new birth, purification from sin, anointing with heavenly power, and entrance into the church (Rom. 6:1–11; Gal. 3:27–28). So, while a baptism ceremony cannot effect or achieve salvation, it is closely linked to our baptism in the Holy Spirit (John 3:5; Titus 3:5).

Communion, like the filling of the Holy Spirit, is experienced again and again. It is a covenant celebration in which God's people look back at the cross to remember Christ's sacrifice and renew our commitment to him (Luke 22:14–20). In the Communion service we also rehearse the great messianic "wedding supper" to come and enjoy a taste of heaven (Rev. 19:9). We eat his body and drink his blood by faith and experience the renewal and forgiveness of the cross (John 6:48–58). Just exactly how Jesus is present in Communion is a mystery that Christians have disagreed about for centuries. But the important thing is that Jesus uses our actions and faith to commune with us and make us more like him.

In the Anaheim Vineyard we regularly invite the Holy Spirit to come and minister to us. And he does—sometimes with spectacular results. He brings forgiveness, healing, and renewal. And he releases spiritual gifts in us, which is the topic of the next chapter.

28

Releasing Gifts in Us

God is at work in the church, manifesting himself through gifts of the Spirit. The purpose of spiritual gifts is the common good of the church (1 Cor. 12:7). The gifts have nothing to do with personal ambition or career orientation. They are not given to build individual reputations, to warrant superior positions in the local church, or to demonstrate spiritual advancement. They are not trophies, but tools. These tools are for touching and blessing others.

Gracelets

In 1 Corinthians 12:8–12 Paul names some of the spiritual gifts that God distributes: words of wisdom, words of knowledge, faith, gifts of healing, miraculous powers, prophecy, the ability to distinguish between spirits, tongues, and interpretation of tongues. Many of us have been taught that this list refers to a one-time, permanent endowment for each person.

But I believe that Paul is not talking here about a dispensing of permanently held spiritual gifts. He is talking about passing touches of the Spirit at different times in different settings. Russell Spittler of Fuller Seminary calls them "gracelets." I like that name. It implies that these are little expressions of God's grace. They come and they go, like fragrant flowers that open and close. In fact, they can come and go in milliseconds. One time a certain gift goes to one person, at another time it goes to another person. At any given time a person could minister in prophecy, in tongues, in healing, or in some other form of blessing for the good of others. Needless to say, that would be hard to accomplish in a church where most members are trained to be passive observers. These are delicate nuances in our relationship with God, and we have to be sensitive enough to respond to them. If we do not, we will never learn to move in the power of the Holy Spirit.

Paul does not give the impression that in the Christian life some people are supposed to be players and others are supposed to be spectators. Christians are all players. Some of us might prefer to be spectators because it is safer just to watch. Sometimes it can be fun to watch because it is a good chance to criticize others. It is easier to be a spectator than a participant. But Paul does not give us that option. He indicates that everyone is to participate.

We are all touched by the Spirit in certain ways at various times, but most of us either have not known that or have not known what to do with it. So it is that many of us have experienced a moving of the Spirit and have suppressed it. For example, when we are suddenly able to apply Scripture to the private life of someone we are talking with, that ability is a spiritual gift. When we walk into a room and suddenly know secret facts about people in the room, that knowledge is a spiritual gift. This is how gifts work. They are manifestations of the Spirit that come on us and work through us. We may not have names for all the gifts, but we can see them functioning. All of us have had a few of these experiences, and we could have more of them if we were encouraged to have them. If we ask for the gifts and seek them, as the Scripture tells us to do, we will get more of them.

One thing that may have prevented us from asking for the gifts is that we have been taught that they are related to personality traits. For example, if a person is always happy, he might be told that his spiritual gift is to be an encourager like Barnabas. Yet some of the best encouragers I know have not been particularly outgoing or positive people. God does give us our unique personalities, so they are, in that sense, gifts from God. But spiritual gifts as I am discussing them are independent of personality traits.

The manifestation of the Spirit is not supposed to be the exception, it is supposed to be the norm. To how many of us does God give spiritual gifts? "To *everyone*." Someone might think, "Not to me. What Paul is talking about hasn't ever happened to me." My answer is "Yes it has! You just didn't have the theology, the practice, or the encouragement to recognize it and respond."

Most of us, frankly, are just too dull and lethargic about our Christian witness and responsibility to be able to release the gifts. Furthermore, many of us are ignorant about spiritual gifts simply because we have not received biblical teaching about them and have not seen healthy examples of them (1 Cor. 12:1). But it is part of the job of apostles, prophets, evangelists, pastors, and teachers to encourage and prod the church to operate in the gifts, and in many places today the church is being encouraged and equipped to learn how to release the spiritual gifts.

Role, Gift, and Ministry

As a young convert, I was often told that I was an evangelist because I led so many people to Christ. But I did not understand about gifts and ministry, and so I denied that I was an evangelist.

"Don't you lead people to Christ?" I was asked.

"Yes—but I thought we were *all* supposed to do that."

I led people to Christ because I thought that witnessing was my duty. But my duty became my passion, and my passion became my ministry. For the first ten years after I became a Christian, evangelizing people was the focal point of my life. Because this is what I was actually doing over and over, it became my ministry. The Spirit bestows a gift and provides the occasions and opportunities for its use: then the repeated use of the gift creates a ministry.

Sheer effort of will often produces works that are naturally good. For example, many people are truly hospitable: generous, warm, kind, and considerate. Their hospitality is a blessing. I think of this as a *role* that all of us are called to. Everyone should anticipate serving in any and all ways, and we should anticipate any and all "gracelets" of the Holy Spirit as we go. So, for example, in our hospitality we may receive a prophetic insight into someone's life and offer it to him or her.

But there are others who have an actual spiritual *gift* of hospitality, an anointing of the Spirit that causes us to leave their homes refreshed spiritually as well as physically. Each of us is likely to discern some area where we characteristically experience particular fruitfulness and unction.

In time a gift evolves into a *ministry*. So, if those with a gift of hospitality exercise it frequently, they soon have the ministry of hospitality. A ministry may or may not be accompanied by formal recognition from church leadership. But that is not crucial. Why? Because our focus is on service to others.

So it is that there is a *role,* a *gift,* and a *ministry*. One can lead to the next, and there is no sharp line of distinction between them.

Like hospitality, intercessory prayer can be a role, a gift, or a ministry. Most of us pray for others as a matter of course, as part of our Christian life. But sometimes there is a supernatural unction, an anointing, that comes upon us to pray for someone in particular. That is the gift of intercessory prayer. A habitual exercise of that gift produces a ministry of intercessory prayer.

Paul has more to say about those who are called to a specific ministry:

> Now you are the body of Christ, and each one of you is a part of
> it. And in the church God has appointed first of all apostles, second
> prophets, third teachers, then workers of miracles, also those having
> gifts of healing, those able to help others, those with gifts of
> administration, and those speaking in different kinds of tongues.
> Are all apostles? Are all prophets? Are all teachers? Do all work

miracles? Do all have gifts of healing? Do all speak in tongues? Do
all interpret? But eagerly desire the greater gifts. (1 Cor. 12:27–31)

I see a distinction between spiritual gifts and ministries. When Paul
asks if all are apostles, prophets, teachers, and miracle workers, his
answer is obviously no. This passage has often been misinterpreted
and understood to be placing a limitation on the abundance of gifts.
But I now see that these verses are Paul's word about church ministries. There should be people in each church appointed by God for
these specific ministries.

For example, if an outstanding work of power takes place in one
of the gatherings in our church, I can usually guess that one of five
or six particular members happened to be praying for the person
who received the miracle. These are the people in our church who
have the ministry of miraculous powers. That is not to say that they
walk around with miracles in their pockets. It is not a matter of apti-
tude. But while they are praying for people with coughs or backaches
or other common ailments, they might come to someone with a far
more significant problem—such as cancer or heart disease—and that
disorder might be healed. We consider that a miracle.

It is the same when it comes to teaching. Some people seem to
be called by God to teach, and they have that ministry. In contrast,
there are many people who simply take on the role of teaching, do
their duty, and do a good job. Not every competent teacher has the
ministry of teaching. When those with the gift teach often enough,
they have the ministry of teaching. It takes time before the gift of
teaching matures and becomes a ministry in the church.

Spiritual gifts are for use anywhere and anytime—in the streets,
marketplace, home, and of course in the church. How they function
in the church is a major concern in the New Testament, and the
topic of the next chapter.

29

Releasing Gifts in the Church

Most of what Scripture tells us about spiritual gifts is in Paul's first Letter to the church in Corinth—in 1 Corinthians 11:17–14:40. There is an interpretative key that is essential to understanding this passage correctly. It is *service to others*.

Like any other church, this one was scattered through the community most of the time and gathered together in meetings at least once a week. Things were not going well in the meetings. When the people came together, they were often rude and thoughtless and some formed exclusive cliques. Some members wolfed down food and drink, some were disorderly, and some took up more than their fair share of the worship time. Paul had to sternly correct this irresponsible behavior.

The parameters of Paul's correction are 1 Corinthians 11:17 and 14:40. He begins the correction by announcing, "your meetings do more harm than good." He ends the correction by advising, "everything should be done in a fitting and orderly way." Between the beginning and the ending of this correction, Paul teaches against divisiveness (he gets sarcastic), misbehavior at the Lord's Supper (he gets profound), and misuse of spiritual gifts (he soars into poetry). The gathered church in Corinth had not been showing the mature concern, caring, and sensitivity appropriate for a body of Christians.

The church at Corinth had spiritual gifts, but they did not understand their purpose and use. I think that is the situation with many Christians today. Just releasing the gifts is such a major step for many of us that we have not yet gone on to learn how to use them in a mature way.

Early in 1 Corinthians 12 Paul writes: "There are different kinds of gifts, but the same Spirit. There are different kinds of service, but same Lord. There are different kinds of working, but the same God works all of them in all men" (vv. 4–6). First Paul says that there are different kinds of gifts. He does not even try to tell us what the various kinds are, because in fact the variety is endless. There is an abundance of gifts, a plethora of gifts. When we think of God's plenitude, munificence, greatness, and magnificence, it is beyond human comprehension and expression. So it is with God's giftings and blessings. They are not countable or categorizable.

Blessing

God expresses his love to all of us in the church by giving us spiritual gifts. And we in turn are to bless each other in the church with the spiritual gifts we receive. This is not wishful thinking or unrealistic theory; it is a matter of awesome but practical fact. The results can often be seen, heard, and touched.

There are, however, two tragic misunderstandings about spiritual gifts. The first is the belief that they do not exist for us today. But Scripture gives no indication that a time would come during the church age in which the gifts would cease. Reliable documents from every century of church history demonstrate that prophecy, healing, deliverance, and tongues have not disappeared from the Christian experience.[1]

The second misunderstanding is the belief that they exist and that they are signs of superiority. Some people think of the gifts as trophies, merit badges, or advanced degrees. They supposedly indicate an elite status in God's sight and a higher level of spirituality. This mistaken point of view might tempt some people to show off their spiritual gifts like karate black belts or Olympic medals. (But Jesus told us what he thought about people showing off their religion.)

One obvious by-product of this idea that the possession of spiritual gifts indicates some kind of superiority is that it divides people into *haves* and *have-nots*. As a result, divisions increase between parts of the body of Christ. People are divided into the Spirit-filled and those who are not Spirit-filled, or the gifted and the ungifted. Then the Spirit-filled can become divided over questions of vocabulary, theory, and the practical uses to which the gifts can be put, differing about how best to minister with gifts such as prophecy, tongues, and interpretation.

I once served as a consultant on a committee concerned about the fact that worshipers in some other churches were singing in tongues. The committee spent the major part of a week forming a statement about the proper use of tongues in church worship, and they ruled out singing. This divided them from members of the body of Christ whose worship included singing in tongues.

It is a tragic irony whenever the gifts of the Spirit, which are given for the common good and for serving others, are used to delineate points of division in this way. I believe that it shows a deep misunderstanding of the nature and meaning of the gifts.

Following the Way of Love

Spiritual gifts are a blessing when they function within the right context. Paul writes:

> And now I will show you the most excellent way.
>
> If I speak with the tongues of men and of angels, but have not love, I am only a resounding gong or a clanging cymbal. If I have the gift of prophecy and can fathom all mysteries and all knowledge, and if I have a faith that can move mountains, but have not love, I am nothing. If I give all I possess to the poor and surrender my body to the flames, but have not love, I gain nothing.

Love is patient, love is kind. It does not envy, it does not boast, it is not proud. It is not rude, it is not self-seeking, it is not easily angered, it keeps no record of wrongs. Love does not delight in evil but rejoices with the truth. It always protects, always trusts, always hopes, always perseveres.

Love never fails. But where there are prophecies, they will cease; where there are tongues, they will be stilled; where there is knowledge, it will pass away. For we know in part and we prophesy in part, but when perfection comes, the imperfect disappears. When I was a child, I talked like a child, I thought like a child, I reasoned like a child. When I became a man, I put childish ways behind me. Now we see but a poor reflection as in a mirror; then we shall see face to face. Now I know in part; then I shall know fully, even as I am fully known.

And now these three remain: faith, hope and love. But the greatest of these is love. (1 Cor. 12:31–13:13)

Love is the essential lubricant that keeps the gifts moving smoothly. Paul is talking to a group of divisive people who have not been practicing love, and he announces that love is the standard. Gifts are not the standard; love is the standard. Love is the highest thing that Jesus has called us to do. It is in the context of our loving one another that gifts will flourish among us.

In my opinion, the highest calling of the renewed church today is to love one another—to love not only the rest of the renewed church, but the whole church, even the part that speaks disparagingly about us. Consider Paul's challenge:

Follow the way of love and eagerly desire spiritual gifts, especially the gift of prophecy. For anyone who speaks in a tongue does not speak to men but to God. Indeed, no one understands him; he utters mysteries with his spirit. But everyone who prophesies speaks to men for their strengthening, encouragement and comfort. He who speaks in a tongue edifies himself, but he who prophesies edifies the church. I would like every one of you to speak in

tongues, but I would rather have you prophesy. He who prophesies
is greater than one who speaks in tongues, unless he interprets, so
that the church may be edified. (1 Cor. 14:1–5)

The first five verses of 1 Corinthians 14 present some severe problems for anyone who still thinks that 1 Corinthians 12:8–12, a list of
gifts, teaches that we are each given only one spiritual gift.

1. Paul tells us to follow the way of love and eagerly desire spiritual gifts (1 Cor. 14:1, 12). That seems nonsensical if God has already
distributed just one gift to each person on a permanent basis (1 Cor.
12:8–10).

2. Paul says he wants everyone to speak in tongues (1 Cor.
14:5). That seems odd if only a few people are to speak in tongues
(1 Cor. 12:10, 30).

3. Paul says he wants everyone to prophesy (1 Cor. 14:5). That
seems strange if only a few people are to prophesy (1 Cor. 12:10, 29).

4. Paul says that sometimes a person who speaks in tongues also
has the gift of interpretation (1 Cor. 14:5, 13). That seems impossible if there is only one gift per person (1 Cor. 12:8–12).

In 1 Corinthians 12 Paul is not talking about one permanent,
exclusive gift that is dealt out to each new Christian like a Social
Security number. The point in 1 Corinthians 12 is that we are meant
to use *all* the transitory, variable gifts of the Holy Spirit for the common good of the gathered church.

Tools, Not Toys

Gifts are not permanent possessions. They are not common talents
or personality traits. Those are also blessings of God, but they are
not spiritual gifts. Spiritual gifts are supernatural manifestations of
the Spirit of God, given momentarily so that God's love, charity,
kindness, and grace may be shed abroad among his people. Paul says,

Since you are eager to have spiritual gifts, try to excel in gifts that
build up the church. . . .

156

> I thank God that I speak in tongues more than all of you. But
> in the church I would rather speak five intelligible words to instruct
> others than ten thousand words in a tongue.
> Brothers, stop thinking like children. In regard to evil be
> infants, but in your thinking be adults. (1 Cor. 14:12, 18–20)

It seems that when people came to church in Corinth, some of them
spoke in tongues, at great length, and with little or no concern
about the rest of the people there. A church that is abusive in the
area of tongues is not a highly spiritual church. It is a church that is
childish. I can understand that when people first experience the gifts
some of them might act in an excessive manner and inconsiderately,
like children with a new toy. But they certainly should not remain
that way. Such people need to learn the ways of God and how to live
and love and function together in maturity.

I greatly treasure the spiritual gifts. It is a shame that there has
often been neglect, misunderstanding, or misuse of the spiritual
gifts—everywhere from Corinth to California, and at every time
from the first century to the twentieth.

Misunderstandings and differing opinions about the gifts of the
Spirit have figured in divisions among Christians, but misunderstandings and divisions do not have to continue. We simply need
more understanding and more maturity.

There is probably no spiritual gift over which people have so frequently been divided as tongues. That is ironic. According to examples in Scripture, tongues plus interpretation always constitute a
message from our spirits to God, exalting him for who he is and
what he has done. In contrast, prophecy is always a message to the
church from God. We can be immensely edified by either one.

Paul claims that if unbelievers come into the church when people are speaking in uninterpreted tongues, they will say that the
believers are out of their minds (1 Cor. 14:23). That has not changed
through the centuries. But if an unbeliever comes in when people
are prophesying, he may be convinced that they are telling the truth
and may discover God there (1 Cor. 14:24–25). In our own church

this has happened repeatedly. Not long ago one of our female church members approached a visitor and told her, in a sensitive way, the secrets of her (the visitor's) heart. As a result, the visitor knew God was speaking to her, was converted, and is now happily settled in our church. I can bear witness that the work of the Spirit that Paul talks about is available in the church today.

Our contemporary prophecies are not to be accorded the same status as Scripture. Today's prophecies—at what could be called the "popular level of prophecy"—are God's repeated messages of strengthening, encouragement, and comfort. They can be prefaced by "Now hear this." They are for the moment. I teach that prophecy today should not be written down and collected; such collections can distract people from the Bible and lead them into heresies. Furthermore, there is not time in a large gathering for everyone who might have a prophecy to give one. If a prophecy is valid and there is not time for it, the person who received it can save it for later.

When I taught a "Signs and Wonders" course at Fuller Seminary, I would ask if anyone present felt an urging from the Holy Spirit to prophesy in this more popular sense. It was not unusual for several students to respond, and the Holy Spirit usually gave them words of strengthening, encouragement, and comfort. Paul's words lead me to believe we should expect prophecy to come in this way:

> What then shall we say, brothers? When you come together, everyone has a hymn, or a word of instruction, a revelation, a tongue or an interpretation. All of these must be done for the strengthening of the church. . . . Therefore, my brothers, be eager to prophesy, and do not forbid speaking in tongues. But everything should be done in a fitting and orderly way. (1 Cor. 14:26, 39–40)

Paul says that in the case of either interpreted tongues or prophecy in church, people should take turns, and only two or three should speak. He is concerned for good order in the church.

Not everything God gives us is spoken publicly to the whole church, because there would not be time for that. More blessings come to more people after our formal service is over than during the service. I often say that most of the teaching, the faith sharpening, the quickening, and the power manifestations take place between the sermon and the car park. That is when the members of the church have more opportunity to minister to each other with the gifts of the Spirit. That is how the gathered church is refreshed and strengthened to go back out into the community again.

In the Western world we have a high view of the value of the individual, but we have little sense of the living reality of a body of people. We sometimes speak of corporate entities, but that is a cold abstraction used in the business world. The Bible tells us that God loves us not only as individuals, but as an intimate group of his children joined sympathetically in warmth and humility, for the honor and glory of God. The gifts are for this entire body.

In a given church body, everyone can partake of the array of spiritual gifts. Then members are also called into particular ministries. Not everyone in a local church will be called to the ministry of evangelism, but a number of people will (Eph. 4:11). Not everyone in a local church will be called to the ministry of healing the sick, but a portion will, and they may function in teams and ministry groups (1 Cor. 12:30). Not everyone in a church will be called to teach, but some will (Eph. 4:11; 1 Cor. 12:29). Everyone has a place of service. We are eagerly to desire the spiritual gifts and be willing to move on into whatever ministries God wants for us. Where churches are coming into this kind of maturity, they are having an increasing influence on the surrounding community.

The gifts of the Spirit are not trophies, talents, traits, or toys. The gifts of the Spirit are God's supernatural expressions of love, caring, kindness, healing, and concern—bestowed upon us and through us.

PART VIII

Fulfilling the
Great Commission

30

The Power of the Gospel

Gunner Payne is a man whose zeal for Jesus motivates him to share the gospel. Back in the late 1950s and early 1960s he went door to door in our town of Yorba Linda, telling virtually every resident about Jesus. Most nights of the week he led evangelistic Bible study groups, patiently answering seekers' questions into the late hours of the night. My wife, Carol, and I were the fruit of one of those Bible study groups.

For the first year of my Christian life I followed Gunner around, learning to do everything he did. Part of that involved telling people about Jesus. I could not go to the market or a hardware store without evangelizing someone. By the end of the year I too was leading evangelistic Bible study groups. Between 1963 and 1970 Carol and I led hundreds of people to Christ, and by 1970 I was leading several Bible study groups a week, with more than five hundred people involved. I was appointed to the staff of Yorba Linda Friends Church in 1970, because we had personally brought so many new Christians into the church.

Through example and teaching, Gunner spliced the value of evangelism into my spiritual "genetic code." Some Christians who know me believe my drive to evangelize is unique. But I do not think it is. *All* Christians should constantly be on the lookout for evangelistic opportunities. Jesus himself preached the gospel throughout his ministry. He commissioned the Twelve (Matt. 10:5–15) and the Seventy-two (Luke 10:1–12) to preach the good news of the kingdom of God, and he now commissions us (Matt. 28:18–20). In Acts 1:8 he promised the disciples, ". . . you will receive power when the Holy Spirit comes on you; and you will be my witnesses in Jerusalem, and in all Judea and Samaria, and to the ends of the earth." Clearly one of the primary purposes of the Holy Spirit is to motivate and empower our witness.

We know that the gospel transforms us as we believe it. But few of us realize that it also transforms us as we *share* it. When we obey God and preach the gospel, *our* faith is built up. In evangelism we are forced to reach out and take risks. In doing so we grow. Sharing our faith, then, is a power point.

Remarkable Insights

Most of the people I led to Christ between 1963 and 1974 came under "normal" circumstances, at least as measured by typical evangelical criteria: I preached the gospel and answered some questions, and they repented and trusted in Jesus.

But occasionally I led someone to Christ in an unusual way. In some instances I received remarkable insights into their lives (for example, knowledge of a specific serious sin or deep hurt). At other times I experienced what seemed like a supernatural anointing of the Holy Spirit going out with my sharing and drawing people to God.[1] God would reveal details of people's lives—their deepest secrets and hurts—that opened them to hearing the gospel.

Yet when I described these experiences to colleagues, they encouraged me not to talk about them. My colleagues were uncomfortable with claims that supernatural phenomena such as signs and wonders were still taking place in the church. (So was I!) They felt I would lose stature if other leaders heard about it. They had no explanation for what happened and, like most of us, they feared the unknown.

In 1974 I left the pastorate to become the founding director of the Department of Church Growth at what is now called the Charles E. Fuller Institute of Evangelism and Church Growth. Over the next four years I introduced several thousand pastors to church growth principles, traveling across America and visiting dozens of denominations. During this time I got to know some Pentecostals. I had previously known little about them, and most of what I did know was inaccurate. Their numbers were growing dramatically, which they attributed to combining proclamation of the gospel with works of power from the Holy Spirit.

Skepticism

Because of my theological background, I was skeptical of their claims about healing. But because of their undeniable growth, I could not write them off. So I visited their bookshops and picked up some of their literature. These writings convinced me that something genuine was going on. And they awakened memories of my earlier, unexplainable evangelistic experiences. It began to dawn on me: Perhaps my experiences were somehow related to the ministry of the Holy Spirit.

While this was going on I was getting involved at Fuller Seminary's School of World Mission, where I served as an adjunct faculty member. I had the honor of coming to know professors like Donald McGavran, Charles Kraft, C. Peter Wagner, and the School of Theology's Russell Spittler. And I was introduced to George Eldon Ladd's writings on the kingdom of God.[2] Their thinking caused me to take a closer look at my theological reservations regarding the Holy Spirit and the charismatic gifts, especially as they were related to evangelism.

Also, at Fuller I met many Third World pastors who reported dramatic instances of signs and wonders and church growth. At first the pastors were quiet about it, but as I probed them they opened up with remarkable stories. I realized that the power of God was at work in the Third World in ways I had not thought possible today.

My earlier unexplained evangelistic encounters paled in comparison with their experiences. At this point I felt compelled to reexamine Scripture, looking more carefully at the relationship between spiritual gifts and evangelism. If this was of God, I reasoned, it had to be biblical.

When I turned to the Bible I tried to answer three questions. First, how did Jesus evangelize? Second, how did Jesus commission the disciples? Third, in the light of their commissioning, how did the disciples evangelize?

How Did Jesus Evangelize?

Jesus, at the beginning of his public ministry, rose in the synagogue in Nazareth, and recited these verses from the prophet Isaiah:

"The Spirit of the Lord is on me,
   because he has anointed me
   to preach good news to the poor.
He has sent me to proclaim freedom
      for the prisoners
   and recovery of sight for the blind,
to release the oppressed,
   to proclaim the year of the
   Lord's favor." (Luke 4:18–19)

Then Jesus stunned his hometown audience by proclaiming, "Today this Scripture is fulfilled in your hearing" (Luke 4:21).

Throughout the Gospels a clear pattern of ministry unfolds, repeated wherever Jesus went. First came *proclamation:* he preached repentance and the good news of the kingdom of God. Second came *demonstration:* he cast out demons, healed the sick, and raised the dead. These signs demonstrated that Jesus was the presence of the kingdom, the Anointed One.

The Gospels occasionally summarize Jesus' ministry. It is particularly interesting to read what Matthew thought was most significant about it:

> Jesus went throughout Galilee, teaching in their synagogues,
> preaching the good news of the kingdom, and healing every disease
> and sickness among the people. News about him spread all over
> Syria, and people brought to him all who were ill with various dis-
> eases, those suffering severe pain, the demon-possessed, those hav-
> ing seizures, and the paralyzed, and he healed them. Large crowds
> from Galilee, the Decapolis, Jerusalem, Judea and the region across
> the Jordan followed him. (Matt. 4:23–25; see also 9:35–36)

Here we see the pattern of proclamation combined with demonstration of the kingdom of God, resulting in large crowds and many
followers.

Another important aspect of Christ's ministry was his emphasis
on the kingdom of God.[3] "Kingdom" is translated from the Greek
word *basileia*, which implies an exercise of kingly rule or reign, rather
than a geographical realm. The kingdom of God is *the dynamic reign
of God*.

Jesus did not consign the kingdom of God to a future millen-
nium. He began his public ministry by announcing, "The kingdom
of God is near. Repent and believe the good news!" (Mark 1:15).
Thus the heart of Jesus' message was both the proclamation of God's
action—"the kingdom is near"—and the demand for a response
from all who heard—"repent and believe."

Jesus demonstrated the presence of the kingdom by healing the
sick, casting out demons, and raising the dead. Every one of his
miracles had a purpose: to confront people with his message that the
kingdom of God had come and that they had to accept or reject it.
This powerful combination of the proclamation and the demonstration of the kingdom was a key to his ministry.

Most people can understand how Jesus was able to preach and
demonstrate the kingdom of God. After all, he was God come in
human form. God heals, casts out demons, and overcomes all forms
of evil. But what about the disciples? How were they able to demonstrate the kingdom of God? And what about us? How can we add
demonstration to our proclamation? The Holy Spirit and his gifts
provide the answer to these questions.

How Did Jesus Commission the Disciples?

For three years Jesus taught the disciples how to minister as he did. He taught them to proclaim and demonstrate the kingdom of God. His postresurrection commission, as recorded in Mark 16:14–20, was consistent with their training:

> Jesus appeared to the Eleven as they were eating; he rebuked them for their lack of faith . . . [and he] said to them, "Go into all the world and preach the good news to all creation. . . . And these signs will accompany those who believe: In my name they will drive out demons; they will speak in new tongues; they will pick up snakes with their hands; and when they drink deadly poison, it will not hurt them at all; they will place their hands on sick people, and they will get well."
>
> . . . Then the disciples went out and preached everywhere, and the Lord worked with them and confirmed his word by the signs that accompanied it.

Many Western Christians are surprised by the emphasis on signs and wonders in this commissioning. Also, the genuineness of Mark 16:9–20 has been challenged on textual grounds. (While it is true that some of the most reliable early manuscripts do not contain this passage, like John 7:53–8:11, it is still included in nearly all Bible versions.) So for the sake of argument, let us discard Mark 16:9–20. Does this really change the nature of our commissioning? Matthew's version reads:

> All authority in heaven and on earth has been given to me. Therefore go and make disciples of all nations, baptizing them in the name of the Father and of the Son and of the Holy Spirit, and teaching them to obey everything I have commanded you. And surely I am with you always, to the very end of the age. (Matt. 28:18–20)

In this passage the Greek word rendered "authority," *exousia,* denotes power that was divinely given to Jesus. Through the indwelling

Holy Spirit we receive the authority of Christ, which is the authority of the Father. "I tell you the truth," Jesus told the Jews who were persecuting him, "the Son can do nothing by himself; he can do only what he sees his Father doing, because whatever the Father does the Son also does" (John 5:19).

Jesus proclaimed and demonstrated the gospel wherever he went, and the apostles did likewise. The early disciples cast out demons, spoke in tongues, and healed the sick. Why is their behavior so difficult for many of us to accept? Why are we always dismissing their behavior as the exception—not the norm—for how we are supposed to live the Christian life? When Jesus commissioned them to make and baptize disciples, the disciples understood that they were to go out and do exactly what Jesus had shown them. How else are we to interpret their subsequent behavior? This leads me to my next point.

How Did the Disciples Respond to the Great Commission?

An old adage goes, "The proof of the pudding is in the eating." This is certainly true of the Great Commission. The book of Acts reveals that the disciples went out and spread the good news in the same fashion as Christ: proclaiming and demonstrating the kingdom of God. Practice is as important as belief, because it communicates our faith. Orthodoxy (right belief) and orthopraxy (right practice) are interrelated, reinforcing and validating each other. The apostles not only taught what they heard, they did what Jesus did.[4]

At the beginning of Acts, Luke wrote that the purpose of his Gospel had been to record all that Jesus did and taught (Acts 1:1). In Acts, Luke continued the story of Jesus' works and teaching—only now they were done by the disciples (Acts 1:8). Clearly he implies that the ministry of the disciples was the continuation of Jesus' ministry on earth, the fulfillment of the Great Commission.

Notice too that power evangelism went beyond the first "generation" of disciples. There were the apostles themselves. Then a second generation, Stephen, Philip, and Ananias—none of them apostles—proclaimed and demonstrated the kingdom (Acts 7; 8:26–40; 9:10–18). Barnabas, Silas, and Timothy represented a *third generation* of those who performed works of power. Finally, from every century of church history we have reliable reports of works of power.[5]

The key to their advancing the kingdom of God was of course the outpouring of the Holy Spirit in Acts 2. When the Spirit came on them the disciples received God's power. Now they were able to do works of power and preach with power. In the next chapter we will take a closer look at how they did it.

31

Proclamation and Demonstration of the Gospel

There are recorded in the book of Acts at least ten kinds of sign phenomena that produced evangelistic growth in the church. They are specifically called "signs and wonders" nine times. They include healing, expelling demons, resuscitation of the dead, speaking in tongues, and being transported from one place to another. Acts 5:12–14 summarizes the disciples' ministry in a fashion similar to Matthew 4:23–25, the passage that summarizes Christ's ministry. It says, "The apostles performed many miraculous signs and wonders among the people. . . . [And] more and more men and women believed in the Lord and were added to their number." In the book of Acts there are fourteen instances where both apostles and others (for example, Stephen) preached, performed works of power, and saw significant church growth.[1]

Even more revealing for me is the contrast in evangelistic results between Paul's work in Athens (Acts 17:16–34) and his work in Corinth (18:1–17). In Athens Paul argued eloquently at the Areopagus, with the result that "A *few* men became followers of Paul and believed" (17:34). In Corinth, the next stop on his apostolic tour,

171

the results were that *"many* who heard him believed and were baptized" (18:8).

While there are several factors that explain the different responses (particularly the different degrees of receptivity found in the people of each city), Paul himself wrote to those in Corinth,

> When I came to you, brothers, I did not come with eloquence or superior wisdom. . . . My message and my preaching were not with wise and persuasive words, but with a demonstration of the Spirit's power, so that your faith might not rest on men's wisdom, but on God's power. (1 Cor. 2:1, 4–5)

It appears that in Corinth Paul combined proclamation with demonstration, as Christ had done throughout his ministry. The word and works of God were coupled in an expression of God's divine will and mercy, culminating in the conversion of individuals as well as groups.

Power Evangelism

The combination of my experiences at Fuller and in the field, plus a rethinking of Scripture, led me to begin praying for the sick. Around this time I returned to the pastorate, leading a small home group that my wife, Carol, had helped start. I have written extensively about my experience in the book *Power Healing,* but one aspect of it bears repeating. I discovered that as people were healed and as I encouraged members of my congregation to pray for the sick (and open themselves up to other works of power), evangelism took off. Put simply, the church exploded. Today we have 5,200 people attending the Anaheim Vineyard and 280 Vineyards (with some 50,000 attendees) scattered across North America.

Properly understood, power evangelism can make all other approaches to evangelism more effective. I define power evangelism as a presentation of the gospel that is rational but which also transcends the rational. The explanation of the kingdom of God comes with a demonstration of God's power. It is a spontaneous, Spirit-inspired presentation of the gospel. It is usually preceded and under-girded by demonstrations of God's presence and frequently results in groups of people being saved. Still, signs and wonders do not save; only Jesus saves. The power for salvation in power evangelism is through the gospel alone. "I am not ashamed of the gospel," Paul writes in Romans 1:16, "because it is the power of God for the salvation of everyone who believes." The content of the gospel, Paul writes elsewhere, is "that Christ died for our sins according to the Scriptures, that he was buried, that he was raised on the third day according to the Scriptures" (1 Cor. 15:3–4).

In power evangelism we do not add to the gospel, nor do we even seek to add power to the gospel. But we do turn to the Third Person of the triune God in our evangelistic efforts, *consciously* cooperating with his anointing, gifting, and leading. Preaching and demonstrating the gospel are not mutually exclusive activities; they work together, reinforcing each other.[2]

Power evangelism is practiced by people who are open to God's power, because Spirit-empowered Christians are living demonstrations of the gospel. Every power point in this book is a means of preparation for power evangelism: thirst for God's word, obeying his voice, touching the Father's heart, living sacrificially, experiencing spiritual gifts, and so on.

But beware: power evangelism puts us in Western culture on a collision course with the way we have been taught to look at the world. We suffer from a "worldview gap" that inhibits our ability to practice power evangelism. In the next chapter we will take a closer look at how worldviews affect evangelism.

32

Kingdoms in Conflict

Virgo Handojo, an Indonesian, was always fascinated by supernatural power. So it was natural that at an early age he became involved with Javanese Kundalini, a form of mysticism rooted in Hinduism and traditional Javanese beliefs. Javanese Kundalini teaches that resident in the spirit of each person is a powerful mother-guardian, and Kundalini strives to awaken and use this power.

"I sought the power and found it," Virgo recently said, "although I now recognize it as demonic. I learned how to communicate with the spirit world. I used black magic. I was able to transport my spirit to other places. I could heal people. I had many mystical experiences."

Then in March 1979 Virgo attended a revival meeting where he heard the gospel. He was attracted to the message, though he made no personal response at the time.

Two days later a friend, who did not know of Virgo's involvement with Kundalini, invited him to a Christian home group meeting. He decided to go. Virgo tells what happened:

> During the meeting a woman had a vision of young people
> involved in black magic. Then the Lord led two people to come
> beside me and lay their hands on my head. I felt something like a
> strong electric current flow through my body. Then a brother said,

"Satan, come out in the name of Jesus!" I felt the evil spirit leave
my body, but it came back immediately. For two hours they strug-
gled to deliver me. It was only when I burned the amulets I had
owned that I felt release from the power of evil.

   The demon tried to return that night, but I cried out to God
to protect me. Then I felt the total presence of God embrace me
with his love. I became a Christian that evening.

When Virgo's family heard what had happened, they were con-
vinced that Jesus was more powerful than any other gods or spirits.
Within three months all eight members of Virgo's family became
Christians.

   Virgo, who as I write this is studying at Fuller Seminary's School
of World Mission, claims that since 1965 millions of Indonesian
Muslims have converted to Christianity. "Some social and political
factors have contributed to this growth," he says, "but the major
stimulus has been supernatural signs and wonders done by the Holy
Spirit through evangelists and church leaders. Power evangelism is
the most effective method for winning Indonesians to Christ."[1]

Naturally Charismatic

Virgo's story is typical of how God is working in many Third World
countries today. C. Peter Wagner offers interesting statistics on
power evangelism's impact on church growth. Latin America, which
in 1900 had only 50 thousand Protestants, now has more than
50 million. Well over three-quarters of these are Pentecostals or
charismatics, and in the last thirty-five years the vast majority have
been converted through power evangelism.[2]

   The fastest growth of Christianity in the history of the world,
Wagner claims, is occurring in China today, through house
churches. When missionaries were driven out in 1950, they left
about 1 million believers who were harshly persecuted. Forty years
later, there are at least 50 million believers in China, and perhaps
twice that number. There are practically no denominations left in

China, but about 85 percent of Chinese Christians (42.5 million) are Pentecostal or charismatic in their belief and practice. Power evangelism also appears to be an integral part of church growth in China.

Recently Don Dunkerley, director of Proclamation International, in Pensacola, Florida, wrote a letter to me in which he quoted Dr. F. Kefa Sempangi, author of *A Distant Grief*, as saying, "African Christians are naturally charismatic." By that he meant that Christians in Africa know demons are real and powerful, but—in the words of Dr. Sempangi—"Jesus is more real and more powerful and he can deliver you from the spirits that have kept you and your ancestors in bondage for centuries." His church, the Redeemed Church in Uganda, grew to 14 thousand in a year and a half. During this time 150 witch doctors became Christians and left their trade. In his letter Dunkerley continues, "In Uganda today the gospel is moving forward in power encounters between Christ and witchcraft."

Anti-supernatural

Why is power evangelism so effective in Third World countries? In part, the answer is that they are more open to spiritual activity of *all* types—good and evil—which means they easily accept supernatural healings, dreams and visions, the existence of demons, and so on. As Don Dunkerley wrote in his letter, "We [in America] don't notice demonized persons, so we don't believe that demons are cast out today by the power of Christ. We have overlooked the entire supernatural dimension, we are unaware of the spiritual warfare that surrounds us."

When those in a Third World country have a demon cast out, as in the case of Virgo Handojo, they do not wonder if they had a psychological breakdown or a hallucination. Their interpretation of supernatural events is supernatural; they look for a spiritual explanation for the experience. When they hear an explanation of the kingdom of God and are converted, their view of reality is altered. They no longer see the world in categories of "natural" and "supernatural"; all of reality is now related to the kingdom of God. In other words, because Virgo is converted to the kingdom of God he sees God's Spirit working in the spirit world. He does not need to be convinced that there is a spirit world. The same holds true for Third World *witnesses* of power evangelism; when they see God's power they too are opened to the gospel. When they convert to the kingdom of God, they see signs and wonders as a natural expression of a new reality.

In Western culture there is skepticism about *anything* spiritual. We are trained to question the supernatural, always looking for alternative explanations for healings, prophecies, evil spirits, and so on. The kingdom of this world says, "The normal manifestations of the kingdom of God—healing, prayer, prophecy—are abnormal, questionable." So we should not be surprised that Great Britain, Western Europe, and North America are not experiencing revival as are other parts of the world today.[3]

Clearly we would be mistaken if we were to limit power evangelism only to non-Western cultures. It is the presence of God's kingdom that makes power evangelism so effective, not a culture's acceptance of supernatural phenomena. But we must not be naive about the challenge of the task of power evangelism in Western culture, for there is a powerful bias against accepting supernatural phenomena as valid today. Even Christians in Western culture question the normal signs of the kingdom of God.

Kingdom Conflict

Ephesians 6:12 says, "For our struggle is not against flesh and blood, but against the rulers, against the authorities, against the powers of this dark world and against the spiritual forces of evil in the heavenly realms." This verse applies to every aspect of the Christian life, including evangelism. People engaged in power evangelism are members of God's army, sent to do battle against the forces of the kingdom of darkness. They *expect* conflict, because they are always looking to overcome the works of Satan in order to set people free.

The difficulty in the Western church is that most of us do not seem to realize there is a war going on. We do not see the relationship that the Bible sees between God and Satan. Due to our secularized, empirical perception of Christian experience, we are unaware that we are living in a world affected by the two kingdoms.

Often we are insensitive to God's kingdom because we are at best only minimally converted to it. We may have repented of our sin and trusted in Christ, but we seem unaware that we are now members of a new kingdom that is opposed to virtually everything the world around us says is important.

This "worldview gap" has led to the erroneous assumption that the spirit world is somehow less real than the tangible, materialistic one in which we live. The spirit world is relegated to myth and superstition.

By accepting the supernatural as a normal part of kingdom living, we consciously encounter Satan's kingdom daily. It is here that we must take on Christ's authority, as given in the Great Commission, to heal diseases and cast out demons, to demonstrate God's reign. How we fight the battle is the topic of the next chapter.

33

How to Fight the Battle

In March 1990 I went with a team to Australia to minister at conferences in Sydney and Perth. Before leaving we sensed that God
wanted to do great things. We also sensed there would most likely be
significant spiritual opposition. So our hundred-member team,
which was drawn from the United States and Canada, began
interceding in earnest for Australia.

Shortly before we left, one of our key leaders, Brent Rue (a Vineyard pastor from Lancaster, California), told me about spiritual
insights that he had gained while praying. Well, actually he heard
from God while *sleeping*. Let me explain. One morning while
interceding Brent became sleepy, and his personal prayer hour
turned into a nap time. However, the Lord gave him a dream that
revealed there is a strong spirit that produces rejection in the nation
of Australia.

Brent could see that this malevolent, invisible force colors the
character of Australia, creating in many people poor self-images,
weakness, and defeat, thus undermining the power of the gospel to
free people to live fully for God.

When Brent told me about his dream I knew that we were about
to be thrust into spiritual warfare. Our battle plans had to be biblical. How were we to respond to a challenge such as this?

Demolishing Strongholds

Scripture teaches that we are called to spiritual warfare. It is critical, though, that we understand the rules of war and what we are fighting against. Paul sheds much light on the nature of spiritual warfare in 2 Corinthians 10:3–6:

> For though we live in the world, we do not wage war as the world does. The weapons we fight with are not the weapons of the world. On the contrary, they have divine power to demolish strongholds. We demolish arguments and every pretension that sets itself up against the knowledge of God, and we take captive every thought to make it obedient to Christ. And we will be ready to punish every act of disobedience, once your obedience is complete.

Paul teaches that we do not wage war as the world does—lining up on opposite sides, fighting, killing one another. We have an alternative means of warfare; we employ different weapons that have "divine power to demolish strongholds," and we fight our battles on a different kind of battlefield.

Where does the battle take place? *In the hearts and minds of men and women.* The strongholds are "arguments and every pretension that sets itself up against the knowledge of God." The Corinthians were receiving false teaching and rejecting Paul's message. What can we learn about spiritual warfare from the Corinthian situation? That there is a battle raging for the hearts and minds of men and women, and Satan knows that if we believe his lies we will fail to love and serve God.

In Colossians 2:8 Paul warns his readers of the influence of "basic principles of this world"—literally in the Greek, "elemental spirits"—on their thinking. We need discernment to avoid being captivated by deceptive philosophy that is based on worldly traditions and elemental spirits. His point raises at least two questions: How do we receive discernment about these spirits? And once we gain discernment, what can we do about it?

Four Steps

First, we ask God for discernment concerning the *nature and activity* of the elemental spirits. When Brent interceded God revealed to him that an elemental spirit in Australia inclines many people—including Christians—to struggle with feelings of rejection and inferiority, which leads to an inability to receive God's grace and acceptance in Christ (Eph. 2:8–10). Simply being aware of this influence helped us focus our prayers and preaching during the two weeks of meetings. If we are open to God and listen for his voice we can be confident that he will speak to us (John 14:26; 16:13–15)—through dreams, visions, as a "still, small voice," and, of course, through Scripture. In other words, he is a *living* God who reigns over the earth and talks to his children. All we have to do is listen.

Second, we ask God to *prepare our hearts and minds* to do the work of the kingdom, and to *prepare the people's hearts and minds* to receive the kingdom. Paul frequently interceded that the early Christians might have discernment:

> And this is my prayer: that your love may abound more and more
> in knowledge and depth of insight, so that you may be able to dis-
> cern what is best and may be pure and blameless until the day of
> Christ, filled with the fruit of righteousness that comes through
> Jesus Christ—to the glory and praise of God. (Phil. 1:9–11)

The twofold strategy behind Paul's prayer is easy to follow. If we are filled with the knowledge of God—and for this to be so we must remain free from sin—then we will recognize the lies of the devil and reject them. And if the people to whom we minister have their spiritual eyes opened to receive God's truth, they will be freed from bondage to deception.

Third, we pray that *God may anoint our preaching and teaching,* and then we preach the truth with boldness. This was what Paul asked the Colossians to do: "And pray for us, too, that God may open a door for our message, so that we may proclaim the mystery of Christ, for which I am in chains. Pray that I may proclaim it clearly, as I should" (Col. 4:3–4). The proclamation of the word of God is the key to winning the hearts and minds of men and women. We demolish Satan's strongholds by living in the light of Scripture and manifesting the wisdom of God (Matt. 12:29; Eph. 3:10). Our prayers, therefore, should focus on asking that the knowledge, insight, and wisdom of God's truth might be proclaimed through us. That is exactly how I prayed for Australia. "Lord, shed the light of the truth of your word wherever we go. Demolish the stronghold of rejection through the clear teaching and the reception of grace."

Finally, the goal of our preaching is that the *people pray, repent, seek God, and humble themselves*. Long ago the Lord told Solomon:

> ". . . If my people, who are called by my name, will humble them-
> selves and pray and seek my face and turn from their wicked ways,
> then will I hear from heaven and will forgive their sin and will heal
> their land. Now my eyes will be open and my ears attentive to the
> prayers offered in this place." (2 Chron. 7:14–15)

These words, spoken to God's people in Old Testament times, apply equally to us. Spiritual battles are won when we act on the truth of the word of God and turn our hearts to him.

Territorial Spirits

Brent's dream points to another aspect of spiritual warfare that Christians are now becoming more aware of: territorial spirits. Territorial spirits are powerful fallen angels—principalities, powers, dominions, thrones, authorities, rulers—who exercise influence over cities, regions, even nations (Eph. 1:21; 6:12; Col. 2:15). They influence every aspect of a culture much as soil types determine which crops can be grown in different regions.

Daniel 10:12–11:1 offers remarkable insight into territorial spirits. It describes two territorial spirits that exercised authority over Persia and Greece—"the prince of the Persian kingdom" and "the prince of Greece" (10:13, 20). Daniel learned of their presence while praying and fasting. Earlier he had received a disturbing revelation about a "great war," and he was seeking further understanding.

In answer to his prayer, God dispatched a messenger—described as "a man" (perhaps a high ranking angel)—who appeared to Daniel in a vision. Daniel was so terrified by the vision that his "face turned deathly pale" (10:8) and he "fell into a deep sleep" (10:9). A "hand" then touched Daniel and "set [him] trembling on [his] hands and knees" (10:10). The messenger told him to stand up and said, "Do not be afraid, Daniel. Since the first day that you set your mind to gain understanding and to humble yourself before your God, your words were heard, and I have come in response to them" (10:12).

The messenger fought for twenty-four days against the prince of Persia. Twenty-one days into the fight the messenger required help from the angel Michael to overcome what most likely was a demon that exercised influence over the Persian realm.

This passage offers two important insights into how we should pray about territorial spirits. First, it teaches that it is *God,* not us, that deploys angels to do spiritual battle. The messenger told Daniel he had come in response to Daniel's prayers to the Father; the Father dispatched the angels. Second, it teaches that God won the battle. On the cross, Christ disarmed the powers and principalities (Col. 2:14–15). In the end, Christ will destroy them (1 Cor. 15:24). When I prayed about Australia I asked *God* to come against the spirit of rejection. If he chose to deploy angels or send his Spirit to bind the territorial spirit, that was his business. My trust is in God and his strategy, not my ideas and efforts.

Our Ultimate Enemy

Cosmic warfare is between fallen and unfallen angels. However, Ephesians 6:12 indicates that *we* engage Satan in combat as well: "For our struggle is not against flesh and blood, but against the rulers, against the authorities, against the powers of this dark world and against the spiritual forces of evil in the heavenly realms."

But I believe that our combat with Satan takes place in a particular way. Paul is describing a struggle in which Satan is our *ultimate* enemy, but not our *immediate* enemy.

Perhaps a brief description of how armies in Paul's day conducted warfare will shed more light on how to interpret this passage. In ancient Near Eastern conflicts, opposing foot soldiers faced each other on a battlefield, with their generals in the rear, overseeing and directing the armies. The generals led through messengers and various signals (flags, hand signals, horns). Everybody fought, but each fought in his own way—foot soldiers, archers, horsemen, messengers, and generals. Now, the ultimate enemy of every foot soldier was the opposing general. But their immediate preoccupation in the midst of battle was with the opposing soldiers.

This is analogous to our situation. We are foot soldiers on a cosmic battlefield, and our ultimate enemy is the evil general, Satan. Under Satan are commanders such as territorial spirits. But we are most likely to have spears thrown at us by his foot soldiers—low-level demons. To deal with these attacks we need, in Paul's words, weapons with "divine power to demolish strongholds" (2 Cor. 10:4). What are these weapons, and how are we to use them?

Defensive Armor

Fortunately, the word of God provides specific instructions about how to fight the war. Ephesians 6:10–18 describes six pieces of armor as analogies for spiritual weapons (plus one other that has no counterpart in Roman armor).

The belt of truth. Putting on God's truth means living out his word—being honest and sincere in our faith, and not full of religious hypocrisy. So the "belt of truth" refers to Christian character and integrity, a life-style that conforms to Scripture.

The breastplate of righteousness. The breastplate protected the soldier's heart. Righteousness is first of all a condition of the heart, and the heart is what determines the course of our lives. The starting point of righteousness is remaining free from sin.

Feet fitted with readiness. We are to be prepared to share the gospel of peace at any time, which means knowing how to tell others about Christ and being open to the Holy Spirit's leading in specific situations.

The shield of faith. The shield protected the soldier against dangerous incendiary missiles. When we take the Great Commission seriously and go on the offensive in challenging Satan's realm, he fights back with flaming arrows. He attacks us and everything associated with us: our church, spouse, children, business—everything. Our shield against these attacks is faith, a belief in God and in his ability to protect us, having confidence in his word.

The helmet of salvation. The helmet, of course, protects the head, the seat of our thought life. Satan bombards us with fear, hatred, suspicion, depression, mistrust, false doctrines, and a host of mental distractions. Thinking Christianly means much more than merely holding right doctrine; it means cultivating the mind of Christ. Our helmet, our protection, is salvation—deliverance from evil and sitting with Christ in heavenly places (Eph. 2:6).

Truth, righteousness, readiness, faith, and assurance of salvation grow and mature as we live devoted and obedient lives that are marked by worshipful hearts, prayerful spirits, and minds conformed to the word of God. This is the defensive armor of spiritual warfare, and without it we are vulnerable to Satan's attack.

Offensive Weapons

Of course, we've been called to more than defense. The last piece of armor—the sword of the Spirit—is designed for both defense and offense. The sword of the Spirit, Paul writes, "is the word of God" (Eph. 6:17). Clearly he is referring primarily to Scripture. But Paul uses language that also can be interpreted to mean a word that is received directly from God and spoken by us. I believe he is referring also to words spoken in the power of the Spirit to assist us in defending ourselves against Satan and in inflicting harm on him.

David Watson points out that the spoken word may come through preaching, teaching, witnessing, or prophesying.[1] To be authentic all words must be in accordance with the written word, and all must glorify the living Word, Jesus. A primary purpose of Jesus' coming is to destroy the work of the devil (1 John 3:8), and he accomplished it through exposing him as the fraud:

> In him [Jesus] was life, and that life was the light of men. The light shines in the darkness, but the darkness has not understood it.
> (John 1:4–5)

Jesus is the truth, the living Word of God; he is light and there is no darkness in him (1 John 1:5). So whatever he came in contact with he exposed—good as from God, and evil as from Satan. This is how he defeated Satan.

In another place Jesus told the disciples, "How can anyone enter a strong man's house and carry off his possessions unless he first ties up the strong man? Then he can rob his house" (Matt. 12:29). For the gospel to bear fruit, Satan must be bound. And Satan is bound by exposing his darkness to the light of God's word! We employed Jesus' "expose-and-conquer" strategy in Australia. Our team went into the enemy's domain in order to begin to take back what the devil had stolen. One of the first things we did was bind the strong man through preaching the truth about God's grace and acceptance and thus exposed the spirit of rejection.

Spiritual Boldness

Paul also mentions another weapon, one that has no counterpart in Roman armor: praying in the Spirit. I mentioned earlier in this chapter that Paul regularly interceded that the believers be filled with the knowledge of God and discernment, for the word of God is the key to destroying satanic strongholds in Christians' lives. But there is another element to intercession that is critical to the defeat of Satan— prayer that God's word may be spoken with boldness and power.

A closer look at the apostles' prayers reveals much about intercession and spiritual warfare. One of the best examples is that of Peter and John in Acts 4. After preaching to the Sanhedrin and receiving threats, they returned to the Jerusalem church and reported what happened to them. Then they called a prayer meeting. They prayed that God might anoint them to "speak your word with great boldness . . . [and] stretch out your hand to heal and perform miraculous signs and wonders . . ." (Acts 4:29–30). God answered their prayers: "After they prayed, the place where they were meeting was shaken. And they were all filled with the Holy Spirit and spoke the word of God boldly" (Acts 4:31). This is the kind of intercessory prayer that will overcome Satan: appealing to God for boldness to fill our mouths with his words and anoint our hands with his deeds. In other words, praying for power evangelism.

Paul continually prayed for boldness, clarity, and opportunity to preach. He also asked others to pray that he would have ample opportunity and clarity in his preaching:

> Pray also for me, that whenever I open my mouth, words may be given me so that I will fearlessly make known the mystery of the gospel. (Eph. 6:19)

Paul's prayer captures the heart of how our team interceded for Australia: "Lord give us opportunity and boldness to preach your word, that we might unmask, disarm, and render powerless the evil lies of the spirit of rejection that have built a stronghold in the hearts and minds of the people."

The Lord answered our prayers for Australia. We preached the gospel with an authority that I have rarely experienced before. Over eighteen thousand people attended the meetings, with hundreds being saved, healed, renewed, and delivered from problems of rejection and defeat. God does truly answer prayer.

We also demonstrate the kingdom of God as we care for the poor and homeless. How we do that is the topic of the last chapter.

34

Caring for the Poor

Social justice is at the very heart of the gospel. Jesus stated his mission in Luke 4:18–19: "to preach good news to the poor, . . . to proclaim freedom for the prisoners and recovery of sight for the blind, to release the oppressed, to proclaim the year of the Lord's favor." In the Old Testament the "year of the Lord's favor" was the year of Jubilee, in which debts were to be remitted, slaves freed, land redistributed (Lev. 25). Jesus announced the impending establishment of an eternal Jubilee.

This was fulfilled in the kingdom that Jesus brought. It is a kingdom in which "justice roll[s] on like a river, [and] righteousness like a never-failing stream" (Amos 5:24), a kingdom that "upholds the cause of the oppressed and gives food to the hungry" and "sets prisoners free" (Ps. 146:7).

Jesus saw the people he preached to and healed as "harassed and helpless" victims of injustice who were powerless to help themselves (Matt. 9:35–36). He linked his healing ministry with ministry to the poor, because he saw both as "bringing justice" (Matt. 11:5; 12:15–21). In the Sermon on the Mount he pronounced blessing on those who hungered and thirsted for justice (Matt. 5:6). Jesus also drew a connection between the kingdom and the command to "love one's neighbor as oneself" (Mark 12:28–34), describing our "neighbors" as those in need and for whom we may have to cross hostile racial barriers (Luke 10:25–37).

Jesus also gave his disciples a clear mandate to act for social justice: "I tell you that unless your righteousness surpasses that of the Pharisees and the teachers of the law, you will certainly not enter the kingdom of heaven" (Matt. 5:20). Obedience to God requires private righteousness and *standing for righteousness in the world* (Matt. 25:31–46).

Justice and Revival

The call to social justice is not "adding to the gospel." It flows from the heart of a God who hates iniquity. The core of the gospel is not concern for social justice, but it certainly provokes that concern. Without that concern, the gospel has not been grasped. That is why social justice goes hand in hand with revival. Great leaders in the history of the church have understood the relationship between the gospel and justice. Consider these examples:

- John Chrysostom (347–407), one of the most powerful preachers in church history, devoted more time and energy to the poor than to preaching. He established many Christian charities, hospices, and hospitals for the destitute.

- Bernard of Clairvaux (1090–1153), the founder of a great monastic movement, led many people to Christ. He also established a network of hostels, hospices, and hospitals that survive today.

- John Wyclif (1329–1384), who translated the New Testament into English, led a grass-roots movement of lay preachers and relief workers who ministered to the poor.

- Dwight L. Moody (1837–1899), best known for his evangelistic ministry, also established more than 150 street missions, soup kitchens, clinics, schools, and rescue outreaches.

Seeking social justice is a mark of true discipleship. But how are we to work for social justice while living under political systems and within social institutions that are so resistant to justice? Here are some of the principles that can guide us.

The Lamb's War

1. *Our primary calling is to a spiritual, not a social or a political, justice.* Before we can go out and fight injustice in the world, justice must personally and corporately live in our hearts. Conquering greed, lust, pride, hate, envy, and fear begins in *us*. Peter writes, "Live such good lives among the pagans that, though they accuse you of doing wrong, they may see your good deeds and glorify God on the day he visits us" (1 Pet. 2:12).

Jesus died on the cross to conquer all forms of injustice *in the world* (John 3:16–17). He left specific instructions for living in a hostile environment: to love our enemies (Matt. 5:43–48); to look after the welfare of others, even those who do evil to us (Matt. 5:39–42); to pray for God's will to be done on earth (Matt. 6:10); to wait for the final judgment in which God will separate believers from nonbelievers.

He did not, however, direct us to form a "Christian state" (Matt. 13:24–30). We may fight to preserve justice and peace in the political order—such as in fighting against poverty or racism—to make the world a more tolerable place in which to live. But we should not confuse the correcting of societal ills with the implementing of the kingdom of God.

Pentecostalism has been one of the greatest forces for social justice in Central and South America in this century. However, David du Plessis, the late Pentecostal spokesman, pointed out that the changes came as a *by-product* of the gospel. Pentecostal missionaries are primarily concerned with correcting spiritual problems, and in doing so social injustice is addressed.

2. *When we fight for justice and peace in the world, evangelism remains our primary mission.* Jesus released the captives by preaching and demonstrating the good news of the kingdom of God wherever he went (Luke 4:18, 43). If our efforts to overcome injustice are detached from spiritual transformation, we are on the road to being taken over by the agenda of the world, for only spiritual transformation addresses the root cause of oppression. The pulling down of evil structures is only a by-product of the presence of the kingdom of God. When people receive the gospel of righteousness, peace, and joy and turn from their injustice, greed, and hate, then—and only then—do we fulfill our call to free the captives.

Ultimately, the most effective way to strike a blow against abortion is to win abortionists to Christ; to fight drug abuse is to win drug dealers to Christ; to combat crooked politics is to win politicians. Then *they* will be salt and light in the world, preaching the gospel and testifying to the spiritual causes of abortion, drug abuse, and crooked politics. In some instances they will change laws that condone abortion, alter social conditions that foster drug abuse, and transform governments that oppress the poor and deny basic civil rights.

Mark Buntain's ministry in India illustrates this principle. In 1953 he started the Calcutta Mission of Mercy, because of the people's initial response to his preaching: "Don't try to give us food for our souls until you give us food for our stomachs." Today their mission feeds twenty-two thousand people a day; it is run by a thousand Indian nationals. The mission also runs a hospital, a school of nursing, village clinics, a hostel for destitute youth, and twelve schools. It has also produced an evangelistic harvest. Four thousand people attend Buntain's church—the Assembly of God in Calcutta—and he preaches to a potential audience of 145 million listeners three times a week over the radio. His work on behalf of the poor is remarkable, but evangelism remains the focus of his ministry.[1]

3. *Seeking social justice is spiritual warfare.* Evil powers, authorities, and institutions are committed to spreading injustice, oppres-

sion, hatred, bigotry, cruelty, tyranny, brutality, and anything else that stands against the kingdom of God (Eph. 6:12). People seeking kingdom justice should *expect* supernatural conflict.

The conflict is intense, but we are equipped with powerful weapons. To understand our weapons we must understand that at the cross Jesus introduced a different kind of warfare. He died for his enemies, to create a people who love their neighbors *and* love their enemies (Rom. 3:21–26; 5:6–11).

We are waging the Lamb's war, a war that Jesus—the Lamb of God—won on the cross. In sacrifice he triumphed over evil. So the cross is the basis for fulfilling Christ's call to justice.

Our weapons have "divine power to demolish strongholds" (2 Cor. 10:3–6). But they are not like modern weapons of military power, political force, or social activism. They are truth, righteousness, readiness, faith, salvation, the word of God, prayer, sacrifice, and love (Eph. 6:10–18; Matt. 16:24; James 2:8).

Powerful weapons are needed to overcome powerful forms of evil. This was illustrated to me by the story of a young girl who attends the weekly Vineyard Lamb's Lunch, a meal and ministry time our church sponsors for over two hundred homeless and impoverished individuals. A few months ago twelve-year-old Susan (not her real name) showed up with a dozen kids in tow. They all lived in a run-down motel. Their parents were in desperate straits. Susan's mother was a heroin addict who disappeared for days at a time.

Susan told Monte Whitaker, the pastor responsible for the Lamb's Lunch, that in the past year nine of her friends had died. "How?" he asked.

"Overdose. Suicide. Shot. Knifed. And . . . you know what rape means?"

"Yes." "Well, they died as a result of being raped. But not me. I've lived."

That week Susan received a warm meal, God's love, and the gospel. She trusted in Jesus, was filled with the Holy Spirit, and has been coming back to the church with other kids from her motel ever since. Susan still has a lot to overcome, but with God's grace and the church's support she has an excellent chance of living a productive life.

Love and Sacrifice

The greatest weapon of all, love, is also our motivation for social justice (1 Cor. 13:13). All of us are familiar with Mother Teresa. For forty-five years she has lived in the slums of Calcutta, ministering to the poorest of the poor. While few of us will ever be called to such sacrifice as Mother Teresa has been, we can learn from her motivation for reaching out to the poor.

Mother Teresa received her calling on September 10, 1946, during a train ride to Darjeeling, India. However, it was not a vision of the poor that motivated her. It was her love of Jesus and obedience to his word. "It [her calling] was a flash of light on the road to Damascus," writes her biographer Edward Le Joly, "a meeting with Jesus, injecting a new spirit and direction to her apostolic life."[2] Jesus is the source of Mother Teresa's motivation. "She obeys His promptings, His direction, without questioning. She does not think of herself, she does everything for Him. And she does it with such complete trust in His power that nothing seems impossible to her. It is all done for God."[3]

At times our sacrifice for the poor means literally losing our lives. This was illustrated to me recently by the death of a Tasmanian missionary to the Philippines. On March 1, 1989, I preached in Melbourne, Australia, on ministry to the poor. As I spoke I sensed that some who answered the call to go out and serve the poor would be martyred, so when I invited them to come forward I mentioned that it might mean their deaths. Some observers report that five hundred young people responded. Two weeks later a woman from Tasmania listened to a tape of my talk and was anointed by the Holy Spirit to minister to prison inmates in the Philippines. She had been preparing for three years, but she did not sense God's anointing until listening to the tape. Her sister later wrote that during the three years of preparation the young missionary had learned the way of the cross, "the way of brokenness so that she was empty of self and full of God."

"Two people," her sister added, "even had visions, one in Sydney, one in Tasmania, that were of her death, yet each did not know the significance of them." In August 1989 the Tasmanian missionary was taken hostage and martyred by inmates in a Philippines prison. Just as Abel "still speaks, even though he is dead" (Heb. 11:4), the suffering of that young missionary remains a powerful witness of the love of God for the hungry, for prisoners, and for the disadvantaged.

It is appropriate that we end *Power Points* with this young missionary's story, because her life sums up the goal of spiritual growth, that we may lose our lives for the glory of God. Her life was not wasted, for, in Paul's words, "to live is Christ and to die is gain" (Phil. 1:21).

AFTERWORD

Last Days Ministry

Could we be entering the period of time immediately preceding the return of Christ? I believe that we could be. According to Scripture, only the Father knows the exact time of Jesus' return (Matt. 24:36). But the conditions for knowing the general time that Jesus taught in passages like Matthew 24:1–51 and Mark 13:1–37 have been met.

Yet despite these clear signs, much of the Western church is not ready for Jesus' return. There are Christians running around who are saying, "Oh, great. Jesus is coming!" But they do not understand that when he returns they will have to stand before a holy Father, a righteous Judge. Their hearts are not ready; they have made no preparations; they have not kept their vows. They have no fear of God.

The nation of Israel was in a situation similar to ours when Amos prophesied back in the mid-eighth century B.C. During this time the Israelites were enjoying great prosperity, military victories, and political success. They were secure and smug, confident that God was pleased with them. They thought of themselves as the people of God, the chosen ones. But they were deceived, for they also practiced idolatry, immorality, oppression of the poor, corruption, and materialism. Because of Israel's sin, God sent Amos to warn them of his impending judgment; he would unleash the full fury of the Assyrians from the north—crushing, capturing, and scattering Israel.

Amos came saying, "Woe to you who long for the day of the Lord! Why do you long for the day of the Lord? That day will be darkness, not light" (Amos 5:18). They were not prepared, so they would be surprised and disappointed. In Scripture light symbolizes grace; darkness judgment. Israel, so confident of being blessed, would be judged severely and harshly. Their minds were dulled, because they had never sought God, submitted to his word, or allowed him to deal with them. They failed to recognize that God was sovereignly blessing them. Instead, they were lulled into spiritual passivity by their success and prosperity. They were so blind that they welcomed the day of the Lord, not recognizing how terrible his judgment of their sin would be.

Thought of in this light, the challenge of spiritual maturity and character growth is especially urgent. Holiness is God's prescription against his coming wrath. For those who are clothed with holiness and purity, he will come as a bridegroom to receive his bride (Rev. 19:7–8). For those who turn their backs on the word of God, it will be a time of sorrow and judgment.

Finally, spiritual maturity is the best preparation for tough times. Western culture is turning its back on its Judeo-Christian roots, and in doing so it is rejecting Jesus Christ . . . and his followers. If mature Christian character is the best (and perhaps the only) way to resist persecution, then it is best built before troubles arise. So think of *Power Points* as a last days training manual.

Hard times are also opportune times, for persecution is almost always accompanied by an evangelistic harvest. But will there be enough mature workers to bring in the harvest? If you take to heart what I have written in this book, perhaps you will be one of those workers. My final challenge to you was spoken long ago by the Lord: "Stand at the crossroads and look; ask for the ancient paths, ask where the good way is, and walk in it, and you will find rest for your souls" (Jer. 6:16).

NOTES

CHAPTER 1. Power Points

1. C. S. Lewis, *Mere Christianity* (New York: Macmillan, 1943), 182–83. Lewis writes, "God became man to turn creatures into sons: not simply to produce better men of the old kind but to produce a new kind of man. . . . [This] is not mere improvement but Transformation."

2. T. C. Hammond, *In Understanding Be Men,* rev. and ed. David F. Wright (Downers Grove, IL: InterVarsity, 1968), 14.

3. William Barclay, *The Letters to Timothy, Titus, and Philemon* (Philadelphia: Westminster, 1960), 100.

CHAPTER 2. Word and Spirit

1. Martyn Lloyd-Jones, *Revival* (Westchester, IL: Crossway Books, 1987), 68.

2. Ibid., 72.

3. Ibid., 72–73.

CHAPTER 3. God in the Desert

1. Leon Morris, *I Believe in Revelation* (Grand Rapids, MI: Eerdmans, 1976), 10.

CHAPTER 5. Special Revelation

1. Also see Ezekiel 7:1; 12:1; Zechariah 8:1; Exodus 4:22; 1 Samuel 2:27.

CHAPTER 6. Why Believe the Bible?

1. This figure based on an August 1988 Gallup Poll, conducted for *The Daily Telegraph* after the Lambeth Conference and reported in the October 1988 issue of *Emerging Trends* (vol. 10, no. 8). It also reported that 40 percent of Catholics and 9 percent of Anglicans in Great Britain attend church frequently—at least once a week or more than once a week. The overall national figure is 14 percent.

A 1984 poll taken in Australia and reported in *Good Weekend* magazine, indicates 22 percent attend church, but the churches themselves estimate only 10 percent attend. (The street poll probably better measures people's intentions than their actions.)

In New Zealand the church attendance figure is similar to England, 9.5 percent.

Overall, Europe is between 5 and 10 percent (some experts think 10 percent is far too high). And these numbers reflect a trend of decline in Christianity since the end of World War II. For example, the May 8, 1989, issue of *National & International Religion Report* (vol. 3, no. 10, p. 6) reports that, in 1989, 46 percent of the Dutch population said they do not belong to a church, compared to 30 percent in 1974. The current population of Europe and Great Britain is about 320 million, which means there are at least 288 million unchurched people! (Most of these figures were provided by Eddie Gibbs of the School of World Mission at Fuller Seminary.)

The June 1988 (vol. 10, no. 6) issue of *Emerging Trends*, published by the Princeton Religion Research Center, reports that in 1988 church attendance among Canadians had fallen to 32 percent. (In 1957, 60 percent of all Canadians regularly attended church.)

2. James I. Packer, *God Speaks to Man* (Philadelphia: Westminster, 1965), 81.

3. Clark H. Pinnock, *Biblical Revelation* (Chicago: Moody, 1971), 51.

CHAPTER 7. The Inspired Word

1. By "Scripture" Paul means not only the Old Testament, but also the New Testament as well. Paul knew that his own writings were Scripture (1 Cor. 14:37), and he puts Luke's Gospel on the same level as the book of Deuteronomy (see 1 Tim. 5:18, where he cites Deut. 25:4 and Luke 10:7 as Scripture). Peter also believed that Paul's writings were Scripture (2 Pet. 3:16).

2. F. F. Bruce, *Commentary on the Book of the Acts* (Grand Rapids, MI: Eerdmans, 1954), 359–60.

3. Charles C. Ryrie, *Basic Theology* (Wheaton, IL: Victor, 1986), 71.

4. Scholars who question divine inspiration handle the Bible in a bizarre and arrogant manner. Their view of inspiration obliges them to stand in judgment of Scripture, determining what is "authentic" and what is a later addition. For example, in 1985 a group of university and seminary professors formed a research group called the "Jesus Seminar" to separate what they thought Jesus actually said from words that may have been put in his mouth by early Christians. Meeting twice yearly, they vote to determine what should be retained and what should be omitted from the Bible. In an October 1988 meeting they voted that all words of the Lord's Prayer except "Father" were not authentic. But, alas, their vote was not unanimous; three scholars said it came from Jesus, six said it probably came from him, ten said it probably did not, and five said it did not. What is not clear is if any of them—even the three who thought it came from Jesus—believe it was God's word. My purpose in reporting on the Jesus Seminar is to emphasize how our view of inspiration affects the way we handle Scripture (Reported in John Dart, "Bible Scholars Say Jesus Didn't Create or Teach Lord's Prayer," *The Los Angeles Times,* October 18, 1988, Part I, p. 3).

5. Clark H. Pinnock, *Biblical Revelation* (Chicago: Moody, 1971), 66–106. I draw from Pinnock's model of inspiration in the following section. I also could have used the outstanding statement drawn from the Lausanne Covenant of 1974:

> We affirm the divine inspiration, truthfulness and authority of both the Old and New Testament Scriptures in their entirety as the only written word of God, without error in all that it affirms, and the only infallible rule of faith and practice. We also affirm the power of God's word to

accomplish His purpose of salvation. The message of the Bible is addressed to all mankind. For God's revelation in Christ and in Scripture is unchangeable. Through it the Holy Spirit still speaks today. He illumines the minds of God's people in every culture to perceive its truth freshly through their own eyes and thus discloses to the whole church ever more of the many-colored wisdom of God.

6. Theologians refer to this as the doctrine of perspicuity.

7. Alfred Rosenberg, *Der Mythus des 20. Jahrhunderts* (Munich: Hoheneichen Verlag, 1934), 599–607. Quoted in Donald G. Bloesch, *The Battle for the Trinity* (Ann Arbor, MI: Servant, 1985), 70.

8. For example, in 1936 the Reich Bishop Mueller revised Matthew 5:4, a verse of the Sermon on the Mount. The Authorized Version reads, "Blessed are they that mourn: for they shall be comforted." Mueller's version reads, "Happy is he who bears his suffering like a man; he will find strength never to despair without courage." See Bloesch, *Battle for the Trinity*, 72. Bloesch took this from Albert Richard Chandler, *Rosenberg's Nazi Myth* (Ithaca, NY: Cornell University Press, 1945), 111.

9. Pinnock, *Biblical Revelation*, 132.

CHAPTER 9. Interpreting God's Word

1. Gordon D. Fee and Douglas Stuart, *How to Read the Bible for All Its Worth* (Grand Rapids, MI: Zondervan, 1982), 16.

2. A few of the more popular and reliable translations are the King James Bible, or the Authorized Version (1611); the American Standard Version (1901); the Revised Standard Version (1946) and the newly revised Revised Standard Version (1990); the New American Standard Bible (1960); and the New International Version (1973).
Paraphrases place greater emphasis on readability for twentieth-century society rather than translating words exactly from the original languages. They are not recommended for serious Scripture study. Examples of paraphrases include the New Testament in Modern English (1958); Good News for Modern Man (1966); and the Living Bible (1971).

3. I recommend the following books to British and American readers: David Alexander and Pat Alexander, eds., *Eerdmans' Handbook to the Bible* (Grand Rapids,

MI: Eerdmans, 1973); J. D. Douglas, ed., *New Bible Dictionary,* 2d ed. (Grand Rapids, MI: Eerdmans, 1982); the *NIV Study Bible* (Grand Rapids, MI: Zondervan, 1985); *Harper's Bible Dictionary* (San Francisco, CA: Harper & Row, 1986).

You should have a concordance that correlates with whatever Bible translation you use. For example, E. W. Goorick and J. R. Kohlenberger III, eds., *The NIV Complete Concordance* (Grand Rapids, MI; Zondervan, 1981) for the New International Version.

4. John White, *Bible Study* (Downers Grove, IL: InterVarsity, 1976), 29.

5. Augustine, *Treatise on the Trinity,* preface.

6. Luther, *Table Talk,* in Theodore G. Tappert, ed., *Luther's Works,* vol. 54 (Philadelphia: Fortress, 1967).

CHAPTER 10. Hearing God's Word

1. David Watson, *Called & Committed* (Wheaton, IL: Harold Shaw, 1982), 105.

2. John 14:9; Hebrews 1:3; Colossians 1:15, 19.

3. The problem of independent, traveling people who stir up significant pastoral problems in congregations is not confined to the prophetic. Traveling teachers, evangelists, and "apostles" who abuse Christians and cause controversy and division are widespread. In this regard, independent prophetic figures are only a part of the bigger problem of individualism in Western Christianity.

CHAPTER 12. One God, Three Persons

1. The belief in many gods is polytheism.

2. The belief that each person of the Godhead is a separate god (not merely a separate person) is tritheism, which is a form of polytheism.

3. Other Old Testament references to the Trinity may include the Angel of Yahweh (Gen. 16:7–13; 18:1–21; 19:1–28; Mal. 3:1); the personification of the word or the wisdom of God (Ps. 33:4, 6; Prov. 8:12–31); where more than one person is mentioned (Pss. 33:6; 45:6, 7; see also Heb. 1:8–9); references to God and the Messiah and/or the Spirit (Isa. 48:16; 61:1; 63:9–10); and threefold liturgical formulas (Num. 6:24–26; Isa. 6:3).

4. Other New Testament references that point in a trinitarian direction include comparing the reference to God as Redeemer and Savior in the Old Testament (Pss. 78:35; 106:21) with references to Christ dwelling among the people of God in their hearts (John 4:42; Gal. 3:13; 4:5; Phil. 3:20; Titus 2:13–14); comparing Yahweh in the Old Testament (Isa. 57:15; Zech. 2:10–11) and the Holy Spirit in the New Testament (Acts 2:4; Rom. 8:9, 11; James 4:5); references to God sending his Son into the world (John 3:16; Gal. 4:4; Heb. 1:6); references to Jesus coming from the Father (John 4:9–10; 8:42; 10:36); references to both the Father and the Son having sent the Holy Spirit (John 14:26; 15:26; 16:7; Gal. 4:6); references to the Father addressing the Son (Mark 1:11; Luke 3:22); references to the Son addressing the Father (Matt. 11:25, 26; 26:39; John 11:41–42; John 12:27–28); the reference to Jesus' assertion of his eternal unity with the Father (John 8:58–59); the reference to Jesus' assertion of his coeternity with the Father (John 17:5); references to the Jews having understood Christ as making himself equal with the Father (John 5:18; 10:33); and references to the Holy Spirit praying to God in the hearts of believers (Rom. 8:26–27). The unity of the Trinity is attested in John 17:20–23 and Ephesians 4:2–6; the Trinity is outlined in 1 Corinthians 12:3–6 and 1 Peter 1:2.

CHAPTER 13. Experiencing the Father's Blessing

1. See Floyd McClung, *The Father Heart of God* (Eastbourne: Kingsway, 1985). McClung is careful to include the significant influence of mothers:

> . . . It is important to emphasize that the Bible says that 'in the image of God he created him, male and female he created them." In other words, both maleness and femaleness are part of God's nature and character, and a full revelation of God's love in the family is not possible unless there is both a father and mother, because they both represent unique aspects of God's character. . . . The norm that God intended was for there to be both a father and mother because *together* they reflect a more complete picture of who God is. (22–23)

See also John White, *Parents in Pain* (Downers Grove, IL: InterVarsity, 1979).

2. For studies on the effects of absent parents on children, see Elyce Wakerman and Holly Barrett, *Father Loss: Daughers Discuss the Man Who Got Away* (New York: Doubleday, 1984); Lenore J. Weitzman, *The Divorce Revolu-

tion: The Unexpected Social and Economic Consequences for Women and Children in America (New York: The Free Press, 1985); and Judith S. Wallerstein and Sandra Blakeslee, *Second Chances* (New York: Ticknor & Fields, 1989).

3. Gary Smalley and John Trent, *The Blessing* (Nashville, TN: Thomas Nelson, 1986), 14.

4. Ibid., 24.

CHAPTER 14. The Parable of the Father's Love

1. Joachim Jeremias, *Rediscovering the Parables* (New York: Scribner, 1966), 101.

2. Floyd McClung, *The Father Heart of God* (Eastbourne: Kingsway, 1985), 39.

CHAPTER 16. Who Do You Say I Am?

1. Hugh J. Schonfield, *The Passover Plot* (New York: Bantam, 1966).

2. Richard N. Ostling, "Who Was Jesus?" *Time,* August 15, 1988.

CHAPTER 17. Fully God

1. The number of Scripture references to Christ's deity is overwhelming. Here are a few of the passages: Matthew 1:23; 28:19; Luke 1:35; 5:20–21; 5:18; Romans 1:4; 2 Corinthians 13:14; Philippians 2:6; Colossians 1:15–20; 2:9; Hebrews 1:3, 8; 2 Peter 1:1; Revelation 1:13–18; 22:13.

2. See Colin Brown, *Miracles and the Critical Mind* (Grand Rapids, MI: Eerdmans, 1988), 197–238.

3. Don Richardson, *Peace Child* (Ventura, CA: Regal, 1976), 211–13.

4. John R. W. Stott, *The Cross of Christ* (Downers Grove, IL: InterVarsity, 1978), 329.

CHAPTER 18. Fully Human

1. Gregory of Nazianzus, *Theological Orations* (A.D. 380), 20–21.

203

CHAPTER 19. Putting On Humility

1. Benjamin B. Warfield, *The Person and Work of Christ* (Philadelphia: Presbyterian and Reformed, 1980), 39–40.

2. F. Kefa Sempangi with Barbara R. Thompson, *A Distant Grief* (Ventura, CA: Regal, 1979), 179.

CHAPTER 20. The Father's Sacrificial Love

1. F. Kefa Sempangi with Barbara R. Thompson, *A Distant Grief* (Ventura, CA: Regal, 1979), 58.

2. Ibid., 149.

3. Ibid., 176.

4. John R. W. Stott, *The Message of Ephesians* (Downers Grove, IL: InterVarsity, 1979), 76.

CHAPTER 22. Recovering Lost Ground

1. D. Martyn Lloyd-Jones, *The Cross* (Westchester, IL: Crossway, 1986), 114.

CHAPTER 23. Sacrificial Living

1. Many of the ideas in this section originally appeared in Jack Deere, "Sacrifice and Power," *Equipping the Saints* (Spring 1990): 9. The material is used by permission of Dr. Deere.

2. Reported in Timothy K. Jones, "Dying for Jesus," *Christianity Today*, March 19, 1990.

CHAPTER 24. Introducing the Holy Spirit

1. R. A. Torrey, *The Person and Work of the Holy Spirit* (Grand Rapids, MI: Zondervan, 1974), 9.

2. In Mark 3:28–30 Jesus refers to blasphemies against the Holy Spirit as sin that "will never be forgiven." The person who sins against the Holy Spirit is "guilty of an eternal sin."

This is a hard word, and it must be taken seriously. What exactly is the "blasphemy against the Holy Spirit"? In Matthew's account (Matt. 12:22–32) Jesus' warning is given to a group of teachers of the law who attributed his healing of a blind and mute man to Satan's power (literally, an "evil spirit") rather than to the Holy Spirit. The teachers had been confronted time and again with Jesus' preaching and demonstration of the kingdom of God, yet they still rejected him and the work of the the Holy Spirit. Finally, in an ultimate act of rebellion, they had the audacity to attribute the works of God to Satan.

Jesus was saying that there comes a point at which people who have seen and heard the gospel so harden their hearts that there is no turning back. Their eternal fates are sealed; God abandons them and gives them over to the desires of their flesh. They are no longer capable of repentance from sin or faith in God.

Rene Pache, *The Person and Work of the Holy Spirit* (Chicago: Moody, 1954), writes, ". . . the sin against the Holy Spirit consists not only of blasphemy against him but also of a voluntary and decisive refusal to allow that work of salvation which he desires to work within us" (60). To blaspheme the Holy Spirit, a person must have an extensive and well-informed religious background to understand the issues surrounding the rejection of the gospel and the attributing of God's works to Satan.

CHAPTER 26. Baptized in the Holy Spirit

1. John R. W. Stott, *Baptism and Fulness,* 2d ed. (Downers Grove, IL: InterVarsity, 1975), 39.

2. D. Martyn Lloyd-Jones, *Joy Unspeakable* (Eastbourne: Kingsway, 1984), 80.

CHAPTER 29. Releasing Gifts in the Church

1. John Wimber with Kevin Springer, *Power Evangelism* (San Francisco: Harper & Row, 1986), 119–21, 157–85.

CHAPTER 30. The Power of the Gospel

1. For an example of one of these instances, see John Wimber with Kevin Springer, *Power Healing* (San Francisco: Harper & Row, 1987), 23–24.

2. Especially see George Eldon Ladd's *A Theology of the New Testament* (Grand Rapids, MI: Eerdmans, 1974); *The Presence of the Future* (Grand Rapids,

MI: Eerdmans, 1974); *Jesus and the Kingdom* (Grand Rapids, MI: Eerdmans, 1964); and *Crucial Questions About the Kingdom of God* (Grand Rapids, MI: Eerdmans, 1952).

3. In fact, I have written a booklet entitled *Kingdom Evangelism* (Ann Arbor, MI: Vine Books, 1989). See also Don Williams, *Signs, Wonders, and the Kingdom of God* (Ann Arbor, MI: Servant, 1989).

4. I am not claiming that the disciples were equal in nature with Jesus. He was God; they (and we) are one with him in the sense that we are regenerated and possess his human nature. The works that we do, we do in the power of the Holy Spirit. Also, I am not claiming that the disciples (or we) do works of power to the degree that Jesus did them. But that the disciples did them at all, that they healed the sick, raised the dead, cast out demons, and—in Peter's case—even walked on water, indicates that we are to do as he did.

5. John Wimber with Kevin Springer, *Power Evangelism* (San Francisco: Harper & Row, 1986), Appendix A ("Signs and Wonders in Church History") and Appendix B ("Signs and Wonders in the Twentieth Century").

CHAPTER 31. Proclamation and Demonstration of the Gospel

1. The following summarizes these instances in the book of Acts:

Works of Power	Preaching	Church Growth
Pentecost (2:4)	Peter (2:14)	3,000 added (2:41)
Cripple healed (3:1)	Peter (3:12)	5,000 believed (4:4)
Miraculous signs (8:6)	Philip (8:6)	Men and women believe (8:12)
Philip appears (8:26)	Philip teaches (8:35)	Eunuch baptized (8:38)
Angel appears, vision Spirit falls (10:3, 12, 44)	Peter (10:34)	Gentiles baptized (10.47)
Lord's hand with them (11:20–21)	Men from Cyprus (11:20)	Many believe (11:21)
Evidence of God's grace (11:23, 24)	Barnabas (11:23)	Great number believe (11:24b)
Holy Spirit falls (13:1–3)	Barnabas, Saul (13:1)	Churches in Asia, Europe
Miraculous signs and wonders (14:1–7)	Paul and Barnabas (14:3)	People divided (14:4, 21–22)

Notes

Works of Power	Preaching	Church Growth
Cripple healed (14:8–18)	Paul and Barnabas (14:15)	Disciples gather (14:21)
Cast out demon (16:16)	Paul and Silas (16:14)	Believers gather (16:40)
Earthquake, prison doors open (16:25, 26)	Paul and Silas (16:31–32)	Jailer and household saved (16:34)
God's power (18:1; cf. 1 Cor. 2:1, 4, 5)	Paul (18:5)	Many believed (18:8)
Extraordinary miracles (19:11–12)	Paul (19:10)	Churches in Asia

2. The term "power evangelism" is also open to much misunderstanding, but I have concluded that the nature of what I am doing will be attacked and misunderstood no matter what it's called; label it what you will, power evangelism is controversial. For example, some draw the wrong conclusion that power evangelism excludes "programmatic evangelism," the hallmark of twentieth-century evangelism. Many fine Christians have devoted their lives to programmatic evangelism—message-centered communication of the gospel primarily through rational arguments. Programmatic evangelism comes in many forms; organized crusades or revivals, door-to-door saturation campaigns in which tracts are presented, media campaigns, personal evangelism contacts, and friendship evangelism are only a few examples. Of course, I am not against programmatic evangelism. Quite the contrary, I endorse and encourage programmatic evangelism.

CHAPTER 32. Kingdoms in Conflict

1. Virgo Handojo's story was taken from C. Peter Wagner, "Researcher's Profile," in Fuller Theological Seminary's *School of World Mission Newsletter* 11.3 (1988), used by permission of Dr. Wagner.

2. C. Peter Wagner, "Church Growth," *Dictionary of Pentecostal and Charismatic Movements,* ed. Stanley M. Burgess and Gary B. McGee (Grand Rapids, MI: Zondervan, 1988), 181–95.

3. The Willowbank Report, *Gospel and Culture* (Lausanne Committee for World Evangelization, 1978) devoted a section to power encounters. It says:

Of course, some are questioning today whether a belief in spirits is compatible with our modern scientific understanding of the universe.

We wish to affirm, therefore, against the mechanistic myth on which the typical Western worldview rests, the reality of demonic intelligences which are concerned by all means, overt and covert, to discredit Jesus Christ and keep people from coming to him. We think it vital in evangelism in all cultures to teach the reality and hostility of demonic powers, and to proclaim that God has exalted Christ as Lord of all and that Christ, who really does possess all power, however we may fail to acknowledge this, can (as we proclaim him) break through any worldview in any mind to make his lordship known and bring about a radical change of heart and outlook.

CHAPTER 33. How to Fight the Battle

1. David Watson, *Called & Committed*, (Wheaton, IL: Harold Shaw, 1982), 107.

CHAPTER 34. Caring for the Poor

1. Scott Shemeth, "Daniel Mark Buntain," *Dictionary of Pentecostal and Charismatic Movements,* ed. Stanley M. Burgess and Gary B. McGee (Grand Rapids, MI: Zondervan, 1988), 101–102.

2. Edward Le Joly, *Servant of Love* (San Francisco: Harper & Row, 1977), 17–18.

3. Ibid., 14.